Manhattan Review

Test Prep & Admissions Consulting

Turbocharge Your SAT: Permutation, Combination & Probability Guide

part of the 2nd Edition Series

April 20th, 2016

☐ *Designed as per the Revised SAT*

☐ *Complete & Challenging Training Sets*

· *Permutation & Combination – 71 Questions*

· *Probability – 69 Questions*

☐ *Mapped according to the scope of the Revised SAT*

☐ *Text-cum-graphic explanation of concepts*

☐ *Ample number of practice questions*

www.manhattanreview.com

Copyright and Terms of Use

10-Digit International Standard Book Number: (ISBN: 1-62926-094-0)
13-Digit International Standard Book Number: (ISBN: 978-1-62926-094-5)

Last updated on April 20th, 2016.

Manhattan Review, 275 Madison Avenue, Suite 1429, New York, NY 10016.
Phone: +1 (212) 316-2000. E-Mail: info@manhattanreview.com. Web: www.manhattanreview.com

About the Turbocharge your SAT Series

The Turbocharge Your SAT Series was created to provide students with comprehensive and highly effective SAT preparation for maximum SAT performance. Thousands of students around the world have received substantial score improvements by using Manhattan Review's SAT prep books. Now in its updated 2nd edition for the new SAT in 2016, the full series of 12 guides is designed to provide SAT students with rigorous, thorough, and accessible SAT instruction for top SAT scores. Manhattan Review's SAT prep books precisely target each testing area and deconstruct the different test sections in a manner that is both student-centered and results-driven, teaching test-takers everything they need to know in order to significantly boost their scores. Covering all of the necessary material in mathematics and verbal skills from the most basic through the most advanced levels, the Turbocharge Your SAT Series is the top study resource for all stages of SAT preparation. Students who work through the complete series develop all of the skills, knowledge, and strategies needed for their best possible SAT scores.

- ☐ **SAT Math Essentials (ISBN: 978-1-62926-090-7)**
- ☐ **SAT Arithmetics Guide (ISBN: 978-1-62926-091-4)**
- ☐ **SAT Algebra Guide (ISBN: 978-1-62926-092-1)**
- ☐ **SAT Geometry Guide (ISBN: 978-1-62926-093-8)**
- ■ **SAT Permutation, Combination & Probability Guide (ISBN: 978-1-62926-094-5)**
- ☐ **SAT Statistics & Data Analysis Guide (ISBN: 978-1-62926-095-2**
- ☐ **SAT Trigonometry & Complex Numbers Guide (ISBN: 978-1-62926-096-9**
- ☐ **SAT Quantitative Question Bank (ISBN: 978-1-62926-097-6**
- ☐ **SAT Sentence Correction Guide (ISBN: 978-1-62926-067-9)**
- ☐ **SAT Critical Reading Guide (ISBN: 978-1-62926-098-3)**
- ☐ **SAT Reading Comprehension Guide (ISBN: 978-1-62926-069-3)**
- ☐ **SAT Writing & Language Test Guide (ISBN: 978-1-62926-099-0)**
- ☐ **SAT Essay Guide (ISBN: 978-1-62926-100-3)**
- ☐ **SAT Vocabulary Builder (ISBN: 978-1-62926-101-0)**

About the Company

Manhattan Review's origin can be traced directly back to an Ivy League MBA classroom in 1999. While teaching advanced quantitative subjects to MBAs at Columbia Business School in New York City, Professor Dr. Joern Meissner developed a reputation for explaining complicated concepts in an understandable way. Prof. Meissner's students challenged him to assist their friends, who were frustrated with conventional test preparation options. In response, Prof. Meissner created original lectures that focused on presenting standardized test content in a simplified and intelligible manner, a method vastly different from the voluminous memorization and so-called tricks commonly offered by others. The new methodology immediately proved highly popular with students, inspiring the birth of Manhattan Review.

Since its founding, Manhattan Review has grown into a multi-national educational services firm, focusing on preparation for the major undergraduate and graduate admissions tests, college admissions consulting, and application advisory services, with thousands of highly satisfied students all over the world. Our SAT instruction is continuously expanded and updated by the Manhattan Review team, an enthusiastic group of master SAT professionals and senior academics. Our team ensures that Manhattan Review offers the most time-efficient and cost-effective preparation available for the SAT. Please visit www.ManhattanReview.com for further details.

About the Founder

Professor Dr. Joern Meissner has more than 25 years of teaching experience at the graduate and undergraduate levels. He is the founder of Manhattan Review, a worldwide leader in test prep services, and he created the original lectures for its first test preparation classes. Prof. Meissner is a graduate of Columbia Business School in New York City, where he received a PhD in Management Science. He has since served on the faculties of prestigious business schools in the United Kingdom and Germany. He is a recognized authority in the areas of supply chain management, logistics, and pricing strategy. Prof. Meissner thoroughly enjoys his research, but he believes that grasping an idea is only half of the fun. Conveying knowledge to others is even more fulfilling. This philosophy was crucial to the establishment of Manhattan Review, and remains its most cherished principle.

International Phone Numbers and Official Manhattan Review Websites

Manhattan Headquarters	+1-212-316-2000	www.manhattanreview.com
USA & Canada	+1-800-246-4600	www.manhattanreview.com
Argentina	+1-212-316-2000	www.review.com.ar
Australia	+61-3-9001-6618	www.manhattanreview.com
Austria	+43-720-115-549	www.review.at
Belgium	+32-2-808-5163	www.manhattanreview.be
Brazil	+1-212-316-2000	www.manhattanreview.com.br
Chile	+1-212-316-2000	www.manhattanreview.cl
China	+86-20-2910-1913	www.manhattanreview.cn
Czech Republic	+1-212-316-2000	www.review.cz
France	+33-1-8488-4204	www.review.fr
Germany	+49-89-3803-8856	www.review.de
Greece	+1-212-316-2000	www.review.com.gr
Hong Kong	+852-5808-2704	www.review.hk
Hungary	+1-212-316-2000	www.review.co.hu
India	+1-212-316-2000	www.review.in
Indonesia	+1-212-316-2000	www.manhattanreview.id
Ireland	+1-212-316-2000	www.gmat.ie
Italy	+39-06-9338-7617	www.manhattanreview.it
Japan	+81-3-4589-5125	www.manhattanreview.jp
Malaysia	+1-212-316-2000	www.review.my
Netherlands	+31-20-808-4399	www.manhattanreview.nl
New Zealand	+1-212-316-2000	www.review.co.nz
Philippines	+1-212-316-2000	www.review.ph
Poland	+1-212-316-2000	www.review.pl
Portugal	+1-212-316-2000	www.review.pt
Qatar	+1-212-316-2000	www.review.qa
Russia	+1-212-316-2000	www.manhattanreview.ru
Singapore	+65-3158-2571	www.gmat.sg
South Africa	+1-212-316-2000	www.manhattanreview.co.za
South Korea	+1-212-316-2000	www.manhattanreview.kr
Sweden	+1-212-316-2000	www.gmat.se
Spain	+34-911-876-504	www.review.es
Switzerland	+41-435-080-991	www.review.ch
Taiwan	+1-212-316-2000	www.gmat.tw
Thailand	+66-6-0003-5529	www.manhattanreview.com
Turkey	+1-212-316-2000	www.review.com.tr
United Arab Emirates	+1-212-316-2000	www.manhattanreview.ae
United Kingdom	+44-20-7060-9800	www.manhattanreview.co.uk
Rest of World	+1-212-316-2000	www.manhattanreview.com

Contents

Chapter 1

Welcome

Dear Students,

Here at Manhattan Review, we constantly strive to provide you the best educational content for standardized test preparation. We make a tremendous effort to keep making things better and better for you. This is especially important with respect to an examination such as the SAT. As you know that from Spring'16, SAT goes for a major change. The revised SAT is challenging now. A typical SAT aspirant is confused with so many test-prep options available. Your challenge is to choose a book or a tutor that prepares you for attaining your goal. We cannot say that we are one of the best, it is you who has to be the judge.

There are umpteen numbers of books on maths for SAT preparation. What is so different about this book? The answer lies in its approach to deal with the questions. The book is meant to develop your fundamentals on one of the most talked about topic on SAT-math—Permutation & Combination and Probability.

The concepts are explained with the help of text-cum-graphic aid. It is a treat to read the book along with relevant graphics. Pictures speak louder than words!

You will find a lot of variety in the problems discussed. Alternate approaches to few tricky questions are worth appreciating. We have tried to rope in the options, a typical SAT test-maker prepares to trap you and duly explained how to get rid of those.

The Manhattan Review's 'New SAT-Permutation & Combination and Probability' book is holistic and comprehensive in all respects. Should you have any queries, feel free to write to us at info@manhattanreview.com.

Happy Learning!

Professor Dr. Joern Meissner
& The Manhattan Review Team

Chapter 2

Introduction to the Revised SAT

The SAT has changed and the Revised SAT will take effect in the Spring of 2016. The revised SAT will comprise two major sections: one, Evidence-based Reading & Writing and two, Math. The essay, which now is optional is excluded from being a compulsory part of SAT Writing section. Evidence-based Reading & Writing has two sections: one, Reading (only Reading, no Critical word prefixed to it, but that does not mean that the new Reading Test will not test critical aspects of reading) and two, Writing & Language Test. This section has gone for a major change in its format. Questions testing your skills at writing, grammar, & language aspects will be taken up from a passage. With both Reading & Writing & Language sections being passage-based, they may also include info-graphics within the passages, and there would be one or two questions based on a graph or a chart. You may have a flavor of some math in the Reading passages & the Writing passages.

While the format of the Math test remains unchanged, there are new additions in Math section. It will focus more on Algebra and Data Analysis. You will see more questions on real-life situational charts and graphs in the test. There is an addition of two new topics: Trigonometry & Complex Numbers. There would be one or two questions testing your higher order thinking. Those questions may be in a set of two questions and would have a lengthy narration. Another special category of questions would be one in which you would be asked to interpret a situation described mathematically in word; there would be four options, each being at least two lines, and only one of the options is correct. Another change to the math section is that there would be a section of No-Calculator.

Two noticeable changes in the Revised SAT are: one, there is no negative marking and two, there would be only four options in MCQs.

Following table does a comparative analysis of The old SAT vs. The revised SAT.

2.1   The Old SAT vs. The Revised SAT

	Old SAT	Revised SAT
Sections	<ul><li>Math</li><li>Critical Reading</li><li>Writing (incl. Essay)</li></ul>	<ul><li>Math</li><li>Evidence-based Reading & Writing<ul><li>Reading</li><li>Writing & Language Test</li></ul></li><li>Essay (optional; exclusive of Writing & Language test)</li></ul>
Content	<ul><li>Reasoning Skills</li><li>Contextual vocabulary</li><li>Applied mathematical problems</li></ul>	<ul><li>Reasoning Skills & knowledge of real-world situations</li><li>Evidence-based Reading, Writing, & Math problems</li><li>Introduction of graphs & charts in passages, thereby testing associated questions (even calculation-based questions)</li><li>Contextual vocabulary in broader contexts</li><li>Introduction of Trigonometry & Complex Numbers in math</li><li>Higher Order thinking questions in math</li></ul>
Question types	<ul><li>Multiple Choice Questions (MCQ)</li><li>Student-produced response Questions (Grid-In) in math</li></ul>	<ul><li>Multiple Choice Questions (MCQ)</li><li>Student-produced response Questions (Grid-In) in math</li></ul>
Number of options for MCQs	5 (A through E)	**4 (A through D)**
Negative marking	$-\frac{1}{4}$ for wrong answer	**No negative marking**

Scoring	• Total score: 600–2400; incl. scores from Critical Reading, Writing, & Math (each score from 200–800) • Writing score includes Essay score	• Total score: 400–1600; incl. scores from Evidence-based Reading and Writing, & Math (each scored from 200–800) • Essays are scored separately (1–4) • Sub-scores & Cross-scores (contribution from selected areas)
Timing	• 3 hours 45 minutes	• 3 hours (excluding essay) • 3 hours 50 minutes (including essay)
Calculator access	Throughout the math section	There would be a No-Calculator section in the math section

2.2 Revised SAT Math content

Content	Topics	Number of questions	
		Calculator	No-Calculator
Heart of Algebra	Fundamental concepts used in Algebra; arranging formulae, linear equations, inequalities, etc.	11	8
Problem Solving & Data Analysis	Understanding qualitative & quantitative data, analyzing relationship, incl. graphical; Ratio & Proportion, Percents, and units of measurements	17	None (All questions with calculator acess)
Passport to Advanced Math	Advanced concepts in Algebra, incl. quadratic & higher order equations, polynomials	7	9
Advanced topics in Math	Geometry (2D, area, volume; & 3D), Trigonometry, Complex numbers	3	3
	Total number of questions (58) **Total time (80 minutes)**	**38** **(55 minutes)**	**20** **(25 minutes)**

Chapter 3

Combinatorics

Combinatorics can be called the **science of counting**. This is the branch of mathematics in which we study the selection and/or the arrangement of the elements of finite sets, having certain characteristics.

We seek to find out the answers to the questions like:

"In how many ways can a team of 4 members be selected from 10 people?"

or

"In how many possible ways can different photographs be taken of a group of people standing in a line, considering that a different order results in a new photograph?"

or

"How many ten-digit phone numbers starting with "98" are possible?"

There are two parts to Combinatorics, namely, **Permutation**, and **Combination**. These can also be called **Counting Methods**.

Combinatorics topic has attracted a fair amount of attention on the SAT recently. It is also a vital topic from the perspective of probability, which is tested on the SAT.

3.1   Permutation

The notion of permutation implies the act of permuting or arranging few objects. Permutation of a set of objects is an act of arranging them in a particular order. For example, there are six possible permutations (arrangements) of the set (A, B, C), namely (A, B, C), (A, C, B), (B, A, C), (B, C, A), (C, A, B), and (C, B, A).

3.2   Combination

The notion of combination is a way of selecting one or several objects out of a set, where the order or the arrangement of objects does not matter. In the above example, selection of all the three objects from the set (A, B, C), namely (A, B, C) is possible in only one way. Arranging the elements as (A, C, B), (B, A, C), (B, C, A), (C, A, B), and (C, B, A) does not make any difference as the same objects are there in each set.

However, if we select only two objects from the set (A, B, C), then there are three possible selections, namely (A, B), (A, C), and (B, C). Sets (B, A), (C, A), and (C, B) do not make a different selection as the order is not important.

Similarly, if we select only one object from the set, then there are three possible selections, namely (A), (B), and (C).

3.3   What's the difference?

We use the word "combination" casually in daily lives, without bothering whether the order of objects is important. Let's see examples.

If I say that the vehicle registration number of my car is formed out of four digits: 0, 2, 5, and 6, can you guess what could be the number? Well, it's not possible to guess correctly as there are many possible numbers out of 0, 2, 5, and 6. If we arrange 0, 2, 5, and 6, there are, for example, 2056, 5602, 6205, and many more numbers. Just for your curiosity, there are as many as 24 possible numbers out of these 4 digits. This calls for **permutation.**

If I say to you that I have three colored balls—red, green, and black. Had it made any difference if I had rather said that I have three colored balls—green, red, and black?—No; as the order in not important. This calls for **combination.**

In other words—*A Permutation is an ordered Combination.*

Combinatorics	Selection is important	Order/Arrangement is important
• Permutation	Yes	Yes
• Combination	Yes	No

3.4 Permutation

Let us develop a formulaic approach to solve lengthy questions.

Question: In how many ways can Alex, Betty, and Chris get photographed?

The foremost decision in the Permutation & Combination based question is to ask which of the two concepts needs to be applied in the question? The answer is: ask yourself whether the arrangement of the objects will render a unique way or a presentation. If the answer is yes, apply permutation, else combination.

In the above question, the arrangement is important as the photograph of Betty, Alex, and Chris (standing in that order) will be different from the photograph of Alex, Betty, and Chris (standing in that order); so, we will apply permutation.

Develop a formula

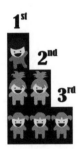

There are a total of three places to be occupied by Alex, Betty, and Chris. They can stand in any order to get photographed. The first place can be occupied in three ways: any one of Alex, Betty, and Chris will stand on the first place; similarly, the second place can be occupied in only two ways as one of Alex, Betty, and Chris has already occupied the first place; and the last place can be occupied in only one way as two of Alex, Betty, and Chris have already occupied the first, and the second place.

So, the **total number of ways = 3 × 2 × 1 = 6 ways.**

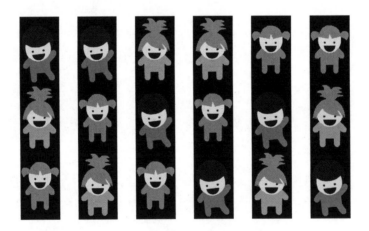

What if there are n number of friends who want to get photographed?

In a similar way, the first place can be occupied in n number of ways: any one of n friends will stand here; similarly, the second place can be occupied in $(n - 1)$ ways as one of n friends has already occupied the first place; similarly, the third place can be occupied in $(n - 2)$ ways as two of n friends have already occupied the first and the second place; and the last place can be occupied in only one way.

So, **the total number of ways $= n \times (n - 1) \times (n - 2) \times (n - 3) \times (n - 4) \times \ldots\ldots\ldots 1 = n!$.**

$n!$ is called factorial n. Its value equals to the product of all the integers from '1' to 'n'.

Selecting few objects from all the objects

Say, if any **two** of Alex, Betty, and Chris are to be photographed, then in how many ways can they be photographed?

Now, there are only two places to be occupied by any two of Alex, Betty, and Chris. The first place can be occupied by 3 ways, and the second place can be occupied by 2 ways.

So, the **total number of ways** = 3 × 2 = **6 ways.**
What if there are r friends out of n friends to get photographed?

On a similar way, the first place can be occupied in n ways; the second place can be occupied in $(n-1)$ ways; the third place can be occupied in $(n-2)$ ways; and similarly, the rth place can be occupied in $(n-r+1)$ or $[n-(r-1)]$ ways.

So, the **total number of ways** = $n \times (n-1) \times (n-2) \times (n-3) \times ....[n-(r-1)]$

In mathematical notations, it is written as P_r^n or $P(n,r)$.

So, $\boldsymbol{P_r^n}$ or $P(n,r) = n \times (n-1) \times (n-2) \times (n-3) \times ....[n-(r-1)]$;

If $r = n$, then P_n^n or $P(n,n) = n \times (n-1) \times (n-2) \times (n-3) \times ....1 = n!$.

If we need to find the permutations of r distinct objects out of n distinct objects, we apply:

$$ P_r^n = \frac{n!}{(n-r)!} \; ; \text{and} \; P_n^n = n! $$

Some most common values of factorials:

- $5! = 5 \times 4 \times 3 \times 2 \times 1 = 120$
- $4! = 4 \times 3 \times 2 \times 1 = 24$
- $3! = 3 \times 2 \times 1 = 6$
- $2! = 2 \times 1 = 2$
- $1! = 1$
- $0! = 1$ (you may by surprised that the value of 0! is '1', but it is so.)

Question: In how many ways can 3 out of 4 friends be photographed?

    Solution: The number of ways = 4.3.2 = 24 ways.

    Formula approach: $n = 4$, and $r = 3$; so, $P_3^4 = \dfrac{4!}{(4-3)!} = \dfrac{4!}{1!} = 4.3.2.1 = 24$ ways.

Question: In how many ways can all 4 friends be photographed?

    Solution: The number of ways = 4! = 4.3.2.1 = 24 ways.

    Formula approach: $n = 4$, and $r = 4$; so, $P_4^4 = \dfrac{4!}{(4-4)!} = \dfrac{4!}{0!} = \dfrac{4.3.2.1}{1} = 24$ ways.

3.4.1 Permutation with repetition of objects

In the examples above, we tried to find out the number ways 3 friends can be photographed. In the example, you must have noticed that each successive place has one less way to get filled. It is because if, say, Betty occupied the first place, she cannot occupy the second or the third place.

Let us see the following example.

Question: How many 3-digit combination codes with digits 1, 2, and 3 are possible for a lock?

> If your answer is 3! = 6 combinations, you assumed that NO digit can be repeated. Say, if the digit '2' occupied the first place, it cannot reappear in the second and the third place.

> However, in a real life, there can be a combination code such as '333', which means that the digits can be repeated.

> So, if the digits can be repeated, the possible number of combinations
> $= 3 \times 3 \times 3 = 27$.

> If there are n digits, and n to be filled, the **total number of ways = n^n**, if repetition is allowed.

Let us see following example.

Question: How many 3-digit passwords are possible with the digits 0, 1, 2 .... 9? Repetition is allowed.

> Since each place can be filled in 10 ways (any digit among 0 to 9 may be used), the total number of possible passwords $= 10 \times 10 \times 10 = 10^3 = 1000$.

> Similarly, for a question: how many r-digit passwords are possible with n digits, if repetition of digits is allowed?

> The answer would be $n \times n \times n \times .... r$ times $= n^r$ passwords.

Number of arrangements out of selecting r objects from n objects = n^r; Repetition is allowed.

Remember that it is important to know beforehand whether repetition is allowed. If it is NOT allowed, then for the above example, the answer would be $P_r^n = \dfrac{n!}{(n-r)!}$.

3.4.2 Circular permutation

We have already seen the question: In how many ways can Alex, Betty, and Chris get seated?

The answer to the question is 3! = 6 ways. It is implied that all three will stand in a row.

What if the question were:

In how many distinct ways can Alex, Betty, and Chris get seated around a <u>round table</u>?

> Well, the answer would be (3 − 1)! = 2! = only 2 ways! This is because, unlike the arrangement in a line, merely by moving from one place to the other does not make a distinct seating arrangement with a round table.
>
> If there are n objects to be arranged in a **circle**, in which all the positions are identical, we need to assign one of the objects to a seat to mark it as the starting point (since in a circle, there is no distinct starting point). Thus, there are $(n - 1)$ objects left to be arranged. So, these n objects can be arranged in $(n - 1)!$ ways.

Let us see how.

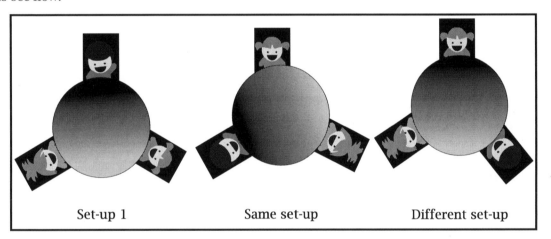

| Set-up 1 | Same set-up | Different set-up |

So, the number of distinct ways n objects can be arranged in a straight line = $n!$;

but,

The number of distinct ways n objects can be arranged around a circle = $(n - 1)!$

3.5 Combination

Let us develop a formulaic approach to solve lengthy questions.

Question: In how many ways can two balls out of three balls (a red, a green, and a black) be selected?

As stated earlier that the foremost decision in the Permutation & Combination based questions is to ask which of the two concepts needs to be applied? Ask yourself whether the arrangement of two balls selected will render a unique selection. If the answer is yes, apply permutation, else combination.

In the above question, the arrangement is not important as, if the two selected balls are, say, red and green, it is does not matter whether they are **red and green** or **green and red**; so, we will apply combination.

Develop the formula

Two balls selected can either be **red and green**, **red and black** or **green and black**, so there are total three ways (RG/RB/GB).

What if the order was given importance, though conceptually wrong in this case, the answer would have been $P_2^3 = 3.2 = 6$ ways (wrong answer).

So, the correct answer can be written as $\dfrac{P_2^3}{2!} = \dfrac{6}{2} = 3$ ways.

So, if r different objects are to be selected out of n different objects, then the total number of ways would be $C_r^n = \dfrac{P_r^n}{r!} = \dfrac{n!}{r!(n-r)!}$

$$\boxed{C_r^n = \dfrac{n!}{r!(n-r)!}}$$

$$\boxed{C_r^n = \dfrac{n.(n-1).(n-2).(n-3).....[n-(r-1)]}{[r.(r-1).(r-2).....1]}}$$

Question: In how many ways can 4 out of 6 balls be drawn from an urn?

Total number of ways $= C_4^6 = \dfrac{6!}{4!(6-4)!} = \dfrac{6!}{4!(2)!} = \dfrac{6.5.4.3.2.1}{(2.1)(4.3.2.1)} = 15$ ways.

Alternate approach 1:

Above approach to calculate the value of C_4^6 is lengthy. It could have been calculated using the following approach. See the next question.

Question: In how many ways can 5 out of 7 balls be drawn from an urn?

Total number of ways $= C_5^7 = \dfrac{7.6.\cancel{5}.\cancel{4}.\cancel{3}}{\cancel{5}.\cancel{4}.\cancel{3}.2.1} = 21$ ways.

Alternate approach 2:

The calculation of C_5^7 can further be simplified; you would have observed that 5, 4, and 3 are getting cancelled from the numerator and the denominator.

However, C_5^7 can be rewritten as $C_{(7-2)}^7$ and is equal to $C_2^7 = \dfrac{7.6}{2.1} = 21$ ways. So,

$$\boxed{C_r^n = C_{(n-r)}^n}$$

But, remember that

$$\boxed{P_r^n \neq P_{(n-r)}^n}$$

Note: Apply Alternate approach 2, if $r > (n-r)$

Question: In how many ways can 2 out of 7 balls be drawn from an urn?

Total number of ways $= C_2^7 = \dfrac{7.6}{2.1} = 21$ ways; however, in this case, we must not transform C_2^7 to $C_{(7-5)}^7$, as this will rather lengthen the calculation, however the answer would be the same.

3.6 Concepts Revisited

Question	Permutation or Combination	Should we apply $C_r^n = C_{(n-r)}^n$?	Solution
In how many ways can 4 out of 6 friends be seated in a row?	**Permutation;** Order is important	Not applicable for permutation	# of ways = 6.5.4.3 = 360 ways
In how many ways can 12 out of 14 players be selected for a team?	**Combination;** Order is not important; only selection the matters.	Yes; as $r > n - r$ $r = 12$ & $n = 14$	# of ways = $C_{12}^{14} = C_2^{14} =$ 14.13/1.2 = 91 ways
In how many ways can 5 different colored balls be arranged in a row to show distinguishable patterns?	**Permutation;** Order is important. Remember that not every question on balls is a combination question.	Not applicable for permutation	# of ways = 5! = 5.4.3.2.1 = 120 ways
In how many ways can 5 different colored balls be arranged around a circle to show distinguishable patterns?	**Circular Permutation;** Order is important	Not applicable for permutation	# of ways = (5 − 1)! = 4! = 4.3.2.1 = 24 ways
In how many ways can 2 out of 6 players be selected for a team?	**Combination;** Order is not important; only the selection matters.	No; $r < n - r$ $r = 2$ & $n = 6$	# of ways = $C_2^6 = 6.5/1.2 =$ 15 ways
In how many ways can all players out of 6 players be selected for a team?	**Combination;** Order is not important; only the selection matters.	Though yes, it is not needed.	For a combination question, if $r = n$ or $r = 0$, # of ways is ALWAYS equal to 1.

3.7 Permutation of multiple indistinguishable objects

Question: How many meaningful or meaningless words can be formed out of the word 'book'?

The answer '4! = 24 words' is a wrong answer as two O's were counted as different letters, but they are the same.

If there are multiple indistinguishable objects, we must exclude the number of ways formed because of them as they are basically the same.

Total number of words = $\dfrac{4!}{2!}$ = 12 words; the 2! in the denominator is for two O's. The 12 words would be **book, boko, bkoo, kboo, kobo, koob, oobk, ookb, okob, obok, obko, & okbo.**

Develop a formula

If there are total n balls, and among these, there are p number of identical green, q number of identical red, and r number of identical black balls, in how many ways can these balls be arranged in a row to have unique patterns?

$$\text{Total number of ways} = \frac{n!}{p!.q!.r!}$$

Question: How many words with or without meaning can be formed out of the word 'Mississippi'?

There are total 11 letters, so $n = 11$; there are four I's, so $p = 4$; four S's, so $q = 4$; two P's, so $r = 2$.

So, total number of words = $\dfrac{11!}{4!.4!.2!} = \dfrac{11!}{2(4!)^2}$ words

3.8   Restricted Permutation

Question: How many 4-digit even numbers can be formed out of digits 0–10? Repetition is allowed.

This is a question on restricted permutation. We not only have to find the count of 4-digit numbers, but also assure that the numbers are even. It implies that the unit digits must be either 0, 2, 4, 6, or 8—only 5 ways; the unit place can be filled in five ways.

Also the digit at the thousandth place cannot be '0', as allowing '0' at the thousandth place will render 3-digit numbers. It implies that the thousandth place digit must be any digit among (1-9): 9 possibilities.

So, total # of 4-digit numbers

= [# of ways to fill thousandth place] × [# of ways to fill hundredth place] × [# of ways to fill tenth place] × [# of ways to fill unit place]

= $9 \times 10 \times 10 \times 5 = 4500$ numbers.

3.9   Restricted Combination

Question: In how many ways can 3 out of 11 players of a team be selected, if the captain must be included in the selection?

Since the captain must be included, the question becomes: In how many ways can 2 out of 10 players of a team be selected?, as one selection (the captain) is already done.

# of ways = $C_2^{10} = 10.9/1.2 = 45$ ways.

If the question is changed to: In how many ways can 3 out of 11 players of a team be selected, provided the captain should NOT be included in the selection?

Since the captain is not to be included, the question becomes: In how many ways can 3 out of 10 players of a team be selected?, as one player (the captain) is out of the selection process.

# of ways = C_3^{10} = 10.9.8/1.2.3 = 120 ways.

Let us see another question with two different set of objects.

Question: In how many ways can a man choose 2 trousers and 3 shirts out of 3 trousers and 4 shirts?

Let's choose trousers first. # of ways to choose trousers = $C_2^3 = C_1^3 = 3$ ways; $[C_r^n = C_{(n-r)}^n]$

Let's choose shirts now. # of ways to choose shirts = $C_3^4 = C_1^4 = 4$ ways;

Total number of ways of choosing 2 trousers and 3 shirts = $3 \times 4 = 12$ ways.

3.10   Rule of Sum

If there are 4 boys and 3 girls, in how many ways can a team of 2 be formed such that there are either both the boys or both the girls in the team?

# of ways 2 boys can be selected = C_2^4 = 4.3/1.2 = 6 ways;

# of ways 2 girls can be selected = $C_2^3 = C_1^3 = 3$ ways;

Since either of the ways can occur, so the total number of ways either two boys or two girls can be selected = 6 + 3 = 9 ways.

The key word is EITHER.

If an event can be done in two or more ways, the numbers of ways are added. This is called **'Rule of Sum'**.

3.11   Rule of Product

If there are 4 boys and 3 girls, in how many ways can a team of 4 be formed such that there must be 2 boys and 2 girls in the team?

# of ways 2 boys can be selected = C_2^4 = 4.3/1.2 = 6 ways;

# of ways 2 girls can be selected = $C_2^3 = C_1^3 = 3$ ways;

Since selecting 4 members is composed of selecting 2 boys and 2 girls, so the total number of ways 4 members would be selected = $6 \times 3 = 18$ ways.

The key word is AND.

If an event is composed of two or more sub-events, total number of ways of doing the event equals to the product of the total number of ways of doing each of the sub-event. This is called **'Rule of Product'**.

Key word	Total # of ways
• Either or	Add the number of ways (+)
• And	Multiply the number of ways (×)

Chapter 4

Practice Questions

Permutation & Combination is a part of **Problem Solving and Data Analysis** of the revised SAT. You will have calculator access for all the questions.

4.1   Multiple Choice Questions

1. 4-digit numbers are formed using the digits 3, 4, 8, and 9. Repetition of digits is allowed. How many of these numbers would be even?

    (A)   56

    (B)   85

    (C)   110

    (D)   128

    Solve yourself:

2. How many different license numbers can be allotted using 3 letters and 3 digits? All the letters and all the digits must appear together. Repetition of the letters and the digits is allowed.

    (A) $C_3^{26}.C_3^{10}$

    (B) $2.C_3^{26}.C_3^{10}$

    (C) $26^3.10^2$

    (D) $2.26^3.10^3$

    Solve yourself:

3. How many 5-digit numbers can be formed containing exactly one '3'? Other digits can be repeated.

    (A) $4.C_4^9$

    (B) $5.C_4^9$

    (C) $4.8.9^4$

    (D) $9^4 + 4.8.9^3$

Solve yourself:

4. There are 8 different locks, with exactly one key for each lock. All the keys have been mixed up. What is maximum number of trials needed to determine which key belongs to which lock?

   (A) 14

   (B) 28

   (C) 56

   (D) 64

   Solve yourself:

5. Captain of a team can select only n players out of $(2n + 1)$ players. If the total number of ways, he can select the players is 126, what is the value of n?

   (A) 2

   (B) 3

   (C) 4

   (D) 5

   Solve yourself:

6. In a polygon of 8 equal sides, how many different triangles can be drawn using the vertices of the polygon as the vertices of the triangles?

   (A) 24

   (B) 28

   (C) 56

   (D) 64

Solve yourself:

7. A puzzle can be solved by choosing 1 cube from the puzzle box1 containing 10 cubes, and 2 cubes from the puzzle box2 containing 5 cubes. In how many ways can the puzzle be solved?

    (A) 50
    (B) 64
    (C) 100
    (D) 128

    Solve yourself:

8. How many numbers less than 1000 can be formed out of digits 3, 4, 5, and 6?

    (A) 16
    (B) 64
    (C) 84
    (D) 128

    Solve yourself:

9. How many 2-member teams can be formed from 5 individuals provided 2 specific individuals together must not be in the team?

    (A) 3
    (B) 6
    (C) 8
    (D) 9

Solve yourself:

10.   In how many ways can 2 boys and 2 girls be chosen from a class comprising 10 boys and 12 girls?

      (A)   111

      (B)   240

      (C)   480

      (D)   2970

      Solve yourself:

11.   How many 5-letter words can be formed if the first letter and the last letter are vowels?

      (A) $2.5^2.26^3$

      (B) $5^2.26^3$

      (C) $5^2.21^3$

      (D) $5^3.21^2$

      Solve yourself:

12.   How many 5-letter codes can be formed out of letters *c, k, m, t, & u* such that no code starts with '*muc* _ _'? Repetition of letters is allowed.

      (A) $5^5 - 3^5$

      (B) $5^5 + 2^5$

      (C) $5^5 - 2^5$

      (D) $5^5 - 5^2$

Solve yourself:

13. A criminal speaks either the truth or the lie for each of three questions. For us to know the fact, he must speak the truth for each question. In how many ways can be hide the truth?

    (A)   2

    (B)   3

    (C)   7

    (D)   8

    Solve yourself:

14. There are 5 differently colored cubes. In how many ways can a child arrange them in a row taking only 3 cubes at a time such that the arrangements make unique patterns?

    (A)   6

    (B)   10

    (C)   15

    (D)   60

    Solve yourself:

15. How many distinct words with or without meaning can be formed using all the letters of the word "APPEALING"?

    (A) $\dfrac{9!}{2!.2!}$

    (B) $\dfrac{9!}{2}$

    (C) $9!$

    (D) $9!.2!.2!$

Solve yourself:

16. In the question given above, how many words will have L and G together (in any order)?

(A) $\dfrac{8!}{2!.2!}$

(B) $\dfrac{8!}{2!}$

(C) $8!$

(D) $\dfrac{9!}{2!.2!}$

Solve yourself:

17. In the question given above, how many words are possible when all the vowels occur together?

(A) 144

(B) 1728

(C) 3456

(D) 4320

Solve yourself:

18. A school wishes to select 11 students for an annual parade out of 15 students with similar height. In how many ways can the school make a selection, if the order of selection does not matter?

(A) 1365

(B) 11!

(C) 1365.(11!)

(D) $(11!)^2$

Solve yourself:

19. UN peacekeeping force wants to form a delegation of 5 generals. It wants to choose 2 out of 5 generals from UK and 3 out of 6 generals from France. In how many ways can the selection be done?

(A) 100

(B) 200

(C) 462

(D) 11!

Solve yourself:

20. A casting director wishes to cast 5 actors out of 13 shortlisted TV actors for his movies. Out of 13 actors, 5 actors act in soaps, and 8 actors act in reality TV shows. In how many ways can the director select the actors such that there are 2 actors from soaps and 3 actors from reality shows?

(A) 110

(B) 356

(C) 560

(D) 6720

Solve yourself:

21. A soccer selection panel has to select 15 probable players out of 17 players such that the captain is always selected and an injured player is not selected. In how many ways can the selection be done?

(A) 15

(B) 120

(C) 136

(D) 560

Solve yourself:

22. How many 3-element subsets of a set {A, B, C, D, E} are possible such that they do not contain the subset of elements A, C, & D?

(A) 5

(B) 6

(C) 9

(D) 50

Solve yourself:

23. A cricket team of 11 players is to be chosen from 8 batsmen, 6 bowlers and 2 wicket-keepers. In how many ways, can the team be chosen if there must be at least 4 batsmen, at least 4 bowlers and exactly 1 wicket-keeper?

(A) 140

(B) 672

(C) 840

(D) 1652

Solve yourself:

24. Number of ways 14 players can be selected out of 25 players is greater that the number of ways 11 players can be selected out of 25 players by:

(A) 0

(B) 3

(C) 25

(D) C_3^{25}

Solve yourself:

25. An urn contains 4 green, 5 red, 6 black, and 7 white balls. What is the minimum number of balls to be drawn from the urn, so that there must be 3 balls of the same color?

(A) 3

(B) 6

(C) 9

(D) 12

Solve yourself:

26. How many seven-digit telephone numbers starting with 2431 are possible, so that the string of the last three digits neither starts nor ends with '0'?

(A) 648

(B) 729

(C) 810

(D) 900

Solve yourself:

27. In how many ways can three men and two women be selected from four men and three women?

(A) 5

(B) 6

(C) 12

(D) 15

Solve yourself:

28. How many three-digit numbers without repetition of digits can be formed using the digits 0, 2, 3, 5 so that they are even?

    (A) 6

    (B) 10

    (C) 15

    (D) 20

    Solve yourself:

29. John has four friends. In how many ways can he invite one or more of his friends to a party?

    (A) 8

    (B) 15

    (C) 16

    (D) 31

    Solve yourself:

30. What is the number of ways in which the letters of the word RANDOM can be arranged in a circle so that the letters A, N, D come together in that order to form 'AND'?

    (A) 2

    (B) 3

    (C) 6

    (D) 8

Solve yourself:

31. What is the number of ways in which the letters of INDIANA be arranged?

    (A)   630

    (B)   700

    (C)   729

    (D)   800

Solve yourself:

32. A 5-member team has to be formed for a debate competition and the speaker for the team has to be decided from among its members. If there are eight members from whom the team has to be picked, in how many ways it can be formed and the speaker is decided?

    (A)   100

    (B)   200

    (C)   280

    (D)   300

Solve yourself:

33. In how many ways can four boys and four girls be seated in a line so that a particular boy and a particular girl do not sit together?

    (A) $6 \times 7!$

    (B) $8! - 7!$

    (C) $12 \times 7!$

    (D) $3 \times 8!$

Solve yourself:

34. A school examination consists of five questions, each having two parts. In how many ways can a student attempt at least one part of any of the questions?

    (A) 624

    (B) 625

    (C) 1023

    (D) 1024

Solve yourself:

35. In how many ways can a person choose between four types of salads and six types of toppings for a pizza?

    (A) 10

    (B) 24

    (C) 48

    (D) 96

Solve yourself:

36. Given that

       A = Number of ways four marbles can be placed in three containers, and

       B = Number of ways three marbles can be placed in four containers

Which of the following statements is correct?

(A) $A = \dfrac{3^4}{4^3} \times B$

(B) $A = \dfrac{4^3}{3^4} \times B$

(C) $A = \dfrac{3}{4} \times B$

(D) $A = B$

Solve yourself:

37. How many four digit numbers less than 2000 can be formed, using the digits '0', '1' and '2', with repetition of digits allowed?

(A)   9

(B)   12

(C)   27

(D)   81

Solve yourself:

38. In how many ways can a team of three members be selected from three men and two women so that at least one woman is always there in the team?

(A)   3

(B)   6

(C)   9

(D)   18

Solve yourself:

39. In how many ways can three boys and three girls be seated in a line so that the boys and girls sit in alternate positions?

(A) 6

(B) 12

(C) 36

(D) 72

Solve yourself:

40. In how many ways can four boys and three girls be seated on a circular table so that a particular boy and girl sit together?

(A) 120

(B) 240

(C) 720

(D) 1440

Solve yourself:

41. In how many ways can one mathematics book from six different mathematics books and one physics book from three identical physics books be selected?

(A) 3

(B) 6

(C) 9

(D) 18

Solve yourself:

42. In how many ways all the letters of the word LATTE can be arranged to form different words so that both T's are together?

(A) 12

(B)   18

(C)   24

(D)   48

Solve yourself:

43.   In how many ways can five friends A, B, C, D and E stand for a photograph such that A stands immediately in front of D?

(A)   12

(B)   24

(C)   48

(D)   60

Solve yourself:

44.   For how many four digit numbers, the digit '0' appears in the tens' position?

(A)   729

(B)   810

(C)   900

(D)   1000

Solve yourself:

45.   In how many ways can one boy and one girl be selected from a group of three boys and two girls?

(A)   3

(B)   6

(C)   8

(D) 9

Solve yourself:

46. Given that

     A = Number of ways 11 players can be selected out of 25 players, and

     B = Number of ways 14 players can be selected out of 25 players

     Which of the following statements is correct?

     (A) $A = \dfrac{14}{11} \times B$

     (B) $A = \dfrac{11}{14} \times B$

     (C) $A = \dfrac{1}{3} \times B$

     (D) $A = B$

     Solve yourself:

47. How many 3-digit even numbers can be formed using the digits 2, 5, 8, and 9, if repetition of digits is allowed.

     (A) 8

     (B) 16

     (C) 32

     (D) 64

     Solve yourself:

48. How many different license numbers can be allotted using 3 letters and 3 digits? All the letters and all the digits must appear together. Repetition of the letters and the digits is allowed.

   (A) $C_3^{26}.C_3^{10}$

   (B) $2.C_3^{26}.C_3^{10}$

   (C) $26^3.10^2$

   (D) $2.26^3.10^3$

   Solve yourself:

49. How many 5-digit numbers can be formed containing exactly one '3'? Other digits can be repeated.

   (A) $4.C_4^9$

   (B) $5.C_4^9$

   (C) $4.9^4 + 9^3$

   (D) $9^4 + 4.8.9^3$

   Solve yourself:

50. In a polygon of 8 equal sides, how many different triangles can be drawn using the vertices of the polygon as the vertices of the triangles?

   (A) 24

   (B) 28

   (C) 56

   (D) 64

   Solve yourself:

51. How many 3-member teams can be formed out of 6 individuals such that one specific individual must be in the team?

(A) 5

(B) 10

(C) 15

(D) 20

Solve yourself:

52. In how many ways can 2-members: either only boys or only girls be chosen from a class comprising 8 boys and 10 girls?

(A) 28

(B) 73

(C) 153

(D) 1260

Solve yourself:

53. How many distinct words (meaningful or meaningless) can be formed using all the letters of the word "BANANA" ?

(A) 9

(B) 60

(C) 120

(D) 720

Solve yourself:

4.2   Student-Produced Response or Grid-In Questions

54.   4-digit numbers are formed using the digits 3, 4, 8, and 9. Repetition of digits is allowed. How many of these numbers would be even?

Solve yourself:

55.   How many triangles can be drawn using of 9 points lying in a plane, if out of these, 3 points are collinear?

Solve yourself:

56.   A puzzle can be solved by choosing 1 cube from puzzle box1 containing 10 cubes, or 2 cubes from puzzle box2 containing 5 cubes. In how many ways can the puzzle be solved?

Solve yourself:

57.   How many numbers between 1 and 9999, inclusive, can be formed out of the digits 0, 1, 2, and 3? Repetition of digits is allowed.

Solve yourself:

58. In how many ways can 2 students be chosen from a class comprising 10 boys and 12 girls?

Solve yourself:

59. There are 6 cubes of different colors. In how many ways can a child arrange them in a circle such that the arrangements make unique patterns?

Solve yourself:

60. How many distinct words (with or without meaning) can be formed using all the letters of the word "LETTER"?

Solve yourself:

61. In the above question, how many distinct words (with or without meaning) can be formed using all the letters of the word "LETTER" such that no two "Es" come together?

Solve yourself:

62. A school wishes to select 11 students out of 15 students for an annual parade. Two students who are far taller than others, while the others are of similar height. In how many ways can the school make a selection of 11 students, if the two taller students must NOT be selected for the parade?

Solve yourself:

63. UN peacekeeping force wants to form a delegation of 5 generals. It wants to choose minimum 1 general out of 5 generals from UK and minimum 2 generals out of 6 generals from France. In how many ways can the selection be done?

Solve yourself:

64. A soccer selection panel has to select 15 probable players out of 18 players such that only one between the captain and the vice-captain is always selected and an injured player is not selected. In how many ways can the selection be done?

Solve yourself:

65. On the Christmas eve, a family of 6 members gifted each other; how many gifts were exchanged?

Solve yourself:

66. On the Christmas eve, a family of 6 members shook hands with each other; how many shake hands took place?

Solve yourself:

67. How many spy-codes are possible taking all the symbols together with the following shapes, if ☐ must be at the beginning?

☐ ▷ ⊗ ⊘ ◇

Solve yourself:

68. How many 4-digit passwords greater than 5999 are possible, using digits 0-9 in the password? A digit can be used only once in the password.

```
┌─┬─┬─┬─┐
│ │ │ │ │
└─┴─┴─┴─┘
```

Solve yourself:

69. In how many ways can 2 boys or 2 girls be chosen from a class comprising 10 boys and 12 girls?

```
┌─┬─┬─┬─┐
│ │ │ │ │
└─┴─┴─┴─┘
```

Solve yourself:

70. How many distinct words with or without meaning can be formed using all the letters of the word "BANANA" such that no two "Ns" come together?

```
┌─┬─┬─┬─┐
│ │ │ │ │
└─┴─┴─┴─┘
```

Solve yourself:

71. How many spy-codes are possible taking all the symbols together with the following shapes such that no codes must have together the □ at the beginning and the ◊ at the end?

□ ▷ ⊗ ⊘ ◊

Solve yourself:

Chapter 5

Answer Key

5.1 Multiple Choice Questions

(1) D

(2) D

(3) D

(4) B

(5) C

(6) C

(7) C

(8) C

(9) D

(10) D

(11) B

(12) D

(13) C

(14) D

(15) A

(16) B

(17) D

(18) A

(19) B

(20) C

(21) A

(22) C

(23) D

(24) A

(25) C

(26) C

(27) C

(28) B

(29) B

(30) C

(31) A

(32) C

(33) A

(34) C

(35) B

(36) A

(37) C

(38) C

(39) D

(40) B

(41) B

(42) C

(43) B

(44) C

(45) B

(46) D

(47) C

(48) D

(49) D

(50) C

(51) B

(52) B

(53) B

5.2 Student-Produced Response or Grid-In Questions

(54) 128

(55) 83

(56) 100

(57) 255

(58) 231

(59) 120

(60) 180

(61) 120

(62) 78

(63) 425

(64) 30

(65) 30

(66) 15

(67) 24

(68) 2016

(69) 111

(70) 40

(71) 114

Chapter 6

Solutions

Permutation & Combination is a part of **Problem Solving and Data Analysis** of the revised SAT. You will have calculator access for all the questions.

6.1 Multiple Choice Questions

1. For a 4-digit number to be even, its unit digit must be either 4 or 8.

   Number of ways, unit place can be filled = 2 (either 4 or 8)

   Number of ways, tenth place can be filled = 4; given that the repetition is allowed.

   Number of ways, hundredth place can be filled = 4

   Number of ways, thousandth place can be filled = 4

   So, total number of ways = 2.4.4.4 = 128 ways.

   The correct answer is option D.

2. Number of ways, each letter can be chosen = 26
   So, total number of ways of choosing 26 letters for three places = 26^3

   Similarly, number of ways, each digit can be chosen = 10
   So, total number of ways of choosing 10 digits for three places = 10^3

   These two blocks of the digits and the letters can be arranged in 2 ways (At the beginning or at the end).

   So, total number of ways = $2.26^3.10^3$ ways.

   The correct answer is option D.

3. '3' can be placed in the following ways in 5-digit numbers: 3XXXX, X3XXX, XX3XX, XXX3X, and XXXX3. Since '3' has to appear only once, we have 9 choices for each vacant place out of digits 0-9 (excluding the digit '3').

   But wait! A 5-digit number cannot begin with a digit '0', so the 5-digit numbers that do not begin with '3' will have only 8 number of ways to its fill ten-thousandth place.

   For numbers X3XXX, XX3XX, XXX3X, and XXXX3, total number of ways = $4.8.9^3$

   For number 3XXXX, total number of ways = 9^4

   Hence, total number of ways = $9^4 + 4.8.9^3$

   The correct answer is option D.

4. We can start with the first key. After maximum 7 number of trials, we can conclude that the last key belongs to the 8th lock. Similarly, for the 2nd key, there would be 6 trails. So, in total trying with all keys, we will need 7+6+5+4+3+2+1 = 28 trials.

    The correct answer is option B.

5. Number of ways n players can be selected out of $(2n + 1)$ players:
    $$C_n^{2n+1} = \frac{(2n + 1)!}{n!.(2n + 1 - n)!}$$
    $$= \frac{(2n + 1)!}{n!.(n + 1)!} = 126 \text{ (Given)}$$

    The better approach to get the value of n would be to plug in values from the options. We recommend that you follow a strategy on which option to try first while plugging in?

    In the question, if the option values are arranged in ascending order, follow B & then D strategy while plugging in.

    Let us try with option B value, $n = 3$, we get $\dfrac{(2n + 1)!}{n!.(n + 1)!} = \dfrac{7!}{3!.4!} = 35$.

    Since the derived value (35) is less than the desired value (126), hence option B or A cannot be the correct answers.

    Let us try with option D value, $n = 5$, we get $\dfrac{(2n + 1)!}{n!.(n + 1)!} = \dfrac{11!}{5!.6!} = 462$.

    Since the derived value (462) is more than the desired value (126), hence option C is the correct answer. We can mark the answer without even trying option C. For the sake of your curiosity, we present to you the value.

    At $n = 4$, $\dfrac{(2n + 1)!}{n!.(n + 1)!} = \dfrac{9!}{4!.5!} = 126$ (desired value)

    The correct answer is option C.

6. A triangle can be drawn taking any 3 vertices of a polygon.

    So, the number of triangles = $C_3^8 = \dfrac{8.7.6}{1.2.3} = 56$

    The correct answer is option C.

    A regular Octagon (8-sided polygon) will not have 3 or more number of co-linear vertices, hence there is no need to think of deducting a few number of dummy triangles formed out of co-linear points.

    What if the question had been:

    How many triangles are possible out of 8 points lying in a plane, out of which 4 points are co-linear?

The answer would not be 56. There would be a few dummy triangles formed out of 4 co-linear points, and we must deduct those from 56.

Number of dummy triangles = $C_3^4 = C_1^4 = 4$

So, total number of genuine triangles = 56 − 4 = 52 triangles

7. Number of ways of choosing 1 cube from Puzzle box1 = $C_1^{10} = 10$

Number of ways of choosing 2 cubes from Puzzle box2 = $C_2^5 = \dfrac{5.4}{1.2} = 10$

Total number of ways = 10.10 = 100

The correct answer is option C.

8. 'Numbers less than 1000' means all 1-digit, 2-digit and 3-digit numbers (1 to 999).

Number of ways of making 1-digit numbers out of 4 digits 3, 4, 5, and 6 = 4.

Number of ways of making 2-digit numbers out of 4 digits 3, 4, 5, and 6 = 4.4 = 16. (Remember that the repetition of digits is allowed. Questions does not restrict us to use the given digits once.)

Number of ways of making 3-digit numbers out of 4 digits 3, 4, 5, and 6 = 4.4.4 = 64.

Total number of ways (Total 'numbers less than 1000') = 4 + 16 + 64 = 84.

The correct answer is option C.

9. Number of ways of choosing 2 members from 5 individuals = $C_2^5 = \dfrac{5.4}{1.2} = 10$.

Since 2 specific individuals **together** must not be in the team, hence the number of ways 2 specific individuals can be chosen = 1.

Hence, the total number of ways = 10−1 = 9.

The correct answer is option D.

Remember that the question asks that the 2 specific individuals **together** must not be in the team, however one of them alone can be a part of the team.

Had you excluded both the individuals while calculating the number of ways, you could have wrongly calculated the answer as $C_2^3 = C_1^3 = 3$.

10. Number of ways of choosing 2 boys out of 10 boys = $C_2^{10} = \dfrac{10.9}{1.2} = 45$

Number of ways of choosing 2 girls out of 12 girls = $C_2^{12} = \dfrac{12.11}{1.2} = 66$

Hence, the total number of ways = 45.66 = 2970.

The correct answer is option D.

11. Number of ways the first place of 5-letter word can be filled (Only vowels) = 5.

Number of ways the second place of 5-letter word can be filled = 26. Remember that the second, third and fourth place can be filled with any letter. **Not only consonants!**

Number of ways the third place of 5-letter word can be filled = 26.

Number of ways the fourth place of 5-letter word can be filled = 26.

Number of ways the fifth place of 5-letter word can be filled (Only vowels) = 5.

Total number of ways = $5^2.26^3$

The correct answer is option B.

12. Number of ways 5 letters can be chosen for 5 places = 5^5

Let us calculate how many 5 letter codes start from *muc _ _?*

To get that, fix first 3 places with letters *m, u, & c.* So, the number of ways 5-letter can be chosen for remaining 2 places = 5^2

Hence, the total number of desired ways = $5^5 - 5^2$

The correct answer is option D.

13. Number of ways he can answer each question = 2
Hence, the number of ways he can answer 3 questions = 2.2.2 = 8

Number of ways he can speak truth for each question = 1
So, the number of ways he can speak truth for 3 questions = 1.1.1 =1

Hence, number of ways he can hide the truth = 8 − 1 = 7

The correct answer is option C.

14. Number of ways 3 cubes can be chosen = $C_3^5 = \dfrac{5.4}{1.2} = 10$

Number of ways 3 chosen cubes can be arranged to present unique pattern = 3! = 3.2.1 = 6

Hence, total number of ways = 10.6 = 60

The correct answer is option D.

This question can either be solved alternatively.

Number of ways 3 cubes can be chosen and arranged = $P_3^5 = 5.4.3 = 60$

15. We know that if there are total n objects, out of these there are p number of one type of identical objects, q number of another type of identical objects, and r number of another type of identical objects, then the number of ways these objects can be arranged in a row to have unique patterns
$= \dfrac{n!}{p!.q!.r!}$

There are total 9 letters; so $n = 9$, and there are 2 Ps and 2 As, so $p = 2$, and $q = 2$.

Thus, the answer is $\dfrac{9!}{2!.2!}$.

The correct answer is option A.

16. Treat L and G as a single object. Though there are total 9 letters, this would imply that there are 8 objects to be arranged in a line. So the total number of words would be $\dfrac{8!}{2!.2!}$. (2 Ps, and 2 As)

However, L and G could interchange their positions as 'LG' or 'GL' in 2! ways.

Thus, the correct answer is $2! \times \left[\dfrac{8!}{2!.2!} \right] = \dfrac{8!}{2!}$

The correct answer is option B.

17. There are 4 vowels (A, A, E, and I) and 5 consonants (P, P, L, N, and G). Treating the vowels as one object, there would be total 6 objects to be arranged in a line. This can be done in $\dfrac{6!}{2!}$ ways (2 P's) and the vowels can be arranged in $\dfrac{4!}{2!}$ ways (2 A's).

Thus, the number of ways = $\dfrac{6!}{2!} \times \dfrac{4!}{2!} = 4320$.

The correct answer is option D.

18. Number of ways 11 students of out 15 can be selected
$= C_{11}^{15} = C_{(15-11)}^{15} = C_4^{15} = \dfrac{15.14.13.12}{1.2.3.4} = 1365$

Note: $C_r^n = C_{n-r}^n$

It is important that the arrangement of 11 students must be ignored as the question states that the order of selection does not matter.

The correct answer is option A.

19. Number of ways 2 generals from 5 UK generals can be selected = $C_2^5 = \dfrac{5.4}{1.2} = 10$

Number of ways 3 generals from 6 French generals can be selected = $C_3^6 = \dfrac{6.5.4}{1.2.3} = 20$

Total number of ways = 10.20 = 200

The correct answer is option B.

20. Number of ways 2 actors from soaps can be selected = $C_2^5 = \dfrac{5.4}{1.2} = 10$

Number of ways 3 actors from reality shows can be selected = $C_3^8 = \dfrac{8.7.6}{1.2.3} = 56$

Total number of ways = 10.56 = 560

The correct answer is option C.

21. Since the captain is to be chosen, the number of players left to be chosen = 15–1 = 14.

Again since the captain is already chosen and the injured player is not to be chosen, number of players left for selection = 17 − 1 − 1 = 15.

Number of ways 14 players can be selected out of 15 players = $C_{14}^{15} = C_1^{15} = 15$.
Note:- $C_r^n = C_{n-r}^n$

The correct answer is option A.

22. Number of ways 3 elements can be selected out of 5 elements = $C_3^5 = \dfrac{5.4.3}{1.2.3} = 10$.

Since the sub-set {A, C, D} is to be excluded, hence the required number of sets = 10 − 1 = 9. Note that in a set, the order or the arrangement of the elements is immaterial.

The correct answer is option C.

23. **Selection 1:** 4 batsmen, 6 bowlers, and 1 wicket-keeper

Number of ways = $C_4^8 . C_6^6 . C_1^2 = C_4^8 . C_0^6 . C_1^2 = \left(\dfrac{8.7.6.5}{1.2.3.4}\right).1.2 = 140$.
Note:- $C_r^n = C_{n-r}^n$ **and** $C_0^n = 1$

Selection 2: 5 batsmen, 5 bowlers, and 1 wicket-keeper

Number of ways = $C_5^8 . C_5^6 . C_1^2 = C_3^8 . C_1^6 . C_1^2 = \left(\dfrac{8.7.6}{1.2.3}\right).6.2 = 672$.

Selection 3: 6 batsmen, 4 bowlers, and 1 wicket-keeper

Number of ways = $C_6^8 . C_4^6 . C_1^2 = C_2^8 . C_2^6 . C_1^2 = \left(\dfrac{8.7}{1.2}\right) \cdot \left(\dfrac{6.5}{1.2}\right).2 = 840$.

Hence, total number of ways = $140 + 672 + 840 = 1652$.

The correct answer is option D.

24. Since the question asks for calculating the number of ways of selecting players, we will apply 'Combination' and not 'Permutation'.

We know that,

Number of ways of selecting r objects out of n objects = $C_r^n = \dfrac{n!}{r!.(n-r)!}$

Thus, number of of ways 11 players can be selected out of 25 players= = $C_{11}^{25} = \dfrac{25!}{11!.(14)!}$

Similarly, number of of ways 14 players can be selected out of 25 players= = $C_{14}^{25} = \dfrac{25!}{14!.(11)!}$

There is no need to calculate values as they are equal, thus the difference is 0.

The correct answer is option A.

25. Since the question asks for minimum number of balls to be drawn from the urn so that we MUST have 3 balls of the same color in hand, we assume ourself unlucky.

Say we happened to draw 2 balls of each color – a total of $2 \times 4 = 8$ balls. The 9th ball, irrespective of what color it is, will give us a set of 3 balls of any color. So the answer is 9 balls.

The correct answer is option C.

What if we were lucky? Well in that case the **minimum** number of balls needed to be drawn would be 3. Say you happened to draw 3 balls of the same color in the first attempt; however this is not a MUST be true scenario.

26. The condition is: the string of the last three digits should not start nor end in '0'.

Thus, the first of the last three digits can be filled using digits from '1' to '9' i.e. 9 ways (excluding '0').
The second of the last three digits can be filled using digits from '0' to '9' i.e. 10 ways (including '0').
The third of the last three digits can be filled using digits from '1' to '9' i.e. 9 ways (excluding '0').

Thus, the number of possible telephone numbers = $9 \times 10 \times 9 = 810$.

The correct answer is option C.

27.   We can select three men from four in $C_3^4 = 4$ ways.

       We can select two women from three in $C_2^3 = 3$ ways.

       Thus, we can select three men AND two women in $C_3^4 \times C_2^3 = 4 \times 3 = 12$ ways.

       The correct answer is option C.

28.   To make a three-digit number, we need to fill up three blank positions using the above digits. Since the number should be even, the last digit should be '0' or '2'.

       Case I: The last digit is '0': _ _ 0

       The first place can be filled using any of '2', '3','5' in three ways.
       The second place can be filled in one less way (since repetition is not allowed) i.e. 2 ways.

       Thus, we can have $3 \times 2 = 6$ such numbers.

       Case II: The last digit is '2': _ _ 2

       The first place can be filled using any of '3' or '5' in two ways (since '0' cannot be used in the first place).
       The second place can be filled in two ways (since zero can be used) i.e. two ways.

       Thus, we can have $2 \times 2 = 4$ such numbers.

       Thus, total # of such numbers = 6 + 4 = 10.

       The correct answer is option B.

29.   John can invite one friend in C_1^4 ways.

       He can similarly invite two or three or all four friends in C_2^4, C_3^4 and C_4^4 ways respectively.

       Thus, number of ways of doing this = $C_1^4 + C_2^4 + C_3^4 + C_4^4 = 4 + 6 + 4 + 1 = 15$.

       Alternatively, we can say that John has two options for each friend: either to call him or not to call him.

       Thus, total number of choices with John = $2 \times 2 \times 2 \times 2 = 16$.

       This includes a case when John invites 'none'. Thus, we need to remove that possibility.

       Hence, total ways = $2^4 - 1 = 15$.

       The correct answer is option B.

30. Since AND must remain intact, we consider it as a single unit. We thus have four objects to be arranged in a circle: (R), (AND), (O) and (M).

This can be done in $(4 - 1)! = 3! = 6$ ways.

The correct answer is option C.

31. INDIANA consists of seven letters of which two are Is, two are Ns and two are As.

Thus, the number of ways in which the letters can be arranged

$$= \frac{7!}{2!2!2!} = \frac{7 \times 6 \times 5 \times 4 \times 3 \times 2 \times 1}{8} = 7 \times 6 \times 5 \times 3 = 630.$$

The correct answer is option A.

32. First we need to select five members from the eight probable members in $C_5^8 = C_3^8$ ways.

Then we need to decide the speaker from the selected five members in C_1^5 ways.

Thus, total number of ways of selecting the team AND deciding the speaker

$$= C_3^8 \times C_1^5 = \frac{8!}{5!.3!} \times 5 = \frac{8!}{4!.3!} = \frac{8 \times 7 \times 6 \times 5 \times 4!}{4!.3!} = 8 \times 7 \times 5 = 280.$$

The correct answer is option C.

33. Let us find the total number of arrangements without any constraint.

Eight people can be seated in 8! ways.

Let us find the number of cases when the particular boy and girl sit together.

We group the two of them as one unit. This results in seven units to be arranged in a line.

Thus can be arranged in 7! ways.

But, for each of the above arrangements, the boy and girl can interchange positions between themselves in 2! ways.

Thus, total number of ways = $7! \times 2!$

Thus, the number of ways when the boy and girl do not sit together

$= 8! - 7! \times 2! = 7!(8 - 2) = 6 \times 7!$

The correct answer is option A.

34. The student has four options for each question: attempt both parts, attempt only the first part, attempt only the second part or leave the question entirely.

Since there are five questions each having four options, total possible options for the student = $4 \times 4 \times 4 \times 4 \times 4 = 4^5$.

Out of these, there is one option where he does not attempt anything which we need to ignore.

Thus, number of possible ways = $4^5 - 1 = 2^{10} - 1 = 1024 - 1 = 1023$.

The correct answer is option C.

35. The person can choose one out of four salads in four ways and one topping out of six toppings in six ways.

Thus, total number of ways of selecting a salad AND a topping = $4 \times 6 = 24$.

The correct answer is option B.

36. Since the question asks for calculating the number of ways of assigning marbles to containers, we will apply 'Permutation' since there can be different ways of assigning marbles to containers.

We know that, number of ways of assigning r objects in n places = n^r

A = # of ways four marbles can be placed in three containers = 3^4.

B = # of ways three marbles can be placed in four containers = 4^3.

Thus, $A = \dfrac{3^4}{4^3} \times B$

The correct answer is option A.

37. Since the question asks for calculating the # of numbers formed using digits, we will apply 'Permutation' since for the same digits, many numbers can be formed by changing the positions of the digits.

Since four digit numbers are to be formed, we need to fill up four blank positions: _ _ _ _.

The first position can be filled up in one way (only possible digit is '1' since the number should be less than 2000).

The second, third and fourth positions can be filled up in three ways each (since each of '0', '1', and '2' can be used).

Thus, total # of such numbers = $1 \times 3 \times 3 \times 3 = 27$.

The correct answer is option C.

---

38. Since the question asks for calculating the number of ways of selecting, we will apply 'Combination' and not 'Permutation'.

We know that, number of ways of selecting r objects out of n objects = $C_r^n = \dfrac{n!}{r!\,(n-r)!}$

Since at least one woman needs to be a part of the team, we have two cases:

  1. Only one woman (from two) and two men (from three): $C_1^2 \times C_2^3 = 2 \times 3 = 6$ ways

  2. Both women (from two) and one man (from three): $C_2^2 \times C_1^3 = 1 \times 3 = 3$ ways

Thus, we have a total of = 6 + 3 = 9 ways.

The correct answer is option C.

39. Since the question asks for calculating the seating arrangements, we will apply 'Permutation'.

We know that, # of ways of arranging n objects in a line = $n!$

The boys and girls can sit in alternate positions in either of the two ways:

  1. B G B G B G

  2. G B G B G B

The three boys and the three girls can be separately arranged in their positions among themselves in 3! = 6 ways each

Thus, total number of ways for each of the cases = $6 \times 6 = 36$ ways.

Thus, total number of ways = $36 \times 2 = 72$ ways.

The correct answer is option D.

40. Since the question asks for calculating the seating arrangements, we will apply 'Permutation'.

We know that, # of ways of arranging n objects in a circle = $(n - 1)!$

We group the particular boy and girl together. Thus, we now have 6 things to arrange in a circle: three boys, two girls and the boy-girl pair.

This can be done in $(6 - 1)! = 5! = 120$ ways.

For each such way, the boy and girl can interchange positions.

Thus, total ways = $120 \times 2 = 240$.

The correct answer is option B.

41. Since the question asks for calculating the number of ways of selecting, we will apply 'Combination' and not 'Permutation'.

We know that, number of ways of selecting r objects out of n objects = $C_r^n = \dfrac{n!}{r!.\,(n-r)!}$

Number of ways of selecting one mathematics book from six different books = C_1^6 = 6 ways.

Number of ways of selecting one physics book from three identical books = 1 way (since there is nothing to choose if the objects are identical; thus, number of identical objects is immaterial.).

Thus, there are a total of $6 \times 1 = 6$ ways.

The correct answer is option B.

42. Since the question asks for calculating the number of ways of forming different words, we will apply 'Permutation' since there can be different ways of arranging the letters of a word to form new words.

Since both T's are to be kept together, we group them as one unit. Thus, there are four things to be arranged.

This can be done in 4! = 24 ways (here, we do not consider the interchanging positions of the two T's since they are identical and hence even on interchanging would give rise to the same situation).

The correct answer is option C.

43. Since the question asks for calculating the number of ways the friends can stand in a line, we will apply 'Permutation'.

We know that, # of ways of arranging n objects in a line = $n!$

Since A stands immediately in front of D, we group A and D as one unit (AD).

Thus, there are four things to be arranged in a line.

This can be done in 4! = 24 ways (here we do not consider the interchanging of A and D since A has to stand in front of D).

The correct answer is option B.

44. Since the question asks for calculating the # of numbers, we will apply 'Permutation' since different numbers can be formed by rearranging the same digits.

In a four digit number, we need to fill up four blanks: _ _ _ _.

Of these, the tens' position has '0'.

The thousands' position can be filled in 9 ways (since the digit '0' cannot be used, as doing so will render 3 digit numbers), the hundreds' position can be filled in 10 ways, and the units' position can be filled in 10 ways.

So, the number of four digit numbers with '0' in the tens' place is $9 \times 10 \times 10 = 900$.

The correct answer is option C.

45. Since the question asks for calculating the number of ways of selecting, we will apply 'Combination' and not 'Permutation'.

We know that, # of ways of selecting r objects out of n objects $= C_r^n = \dfrac{n!}{r!\,(n-r)!}$

We can select one boy from three boys in $C_1^3 = 3$ ways.

We can select one girl from two girls in $C_1^2 = 2$ ways.

Since we need to select one boy AND one girl, total number of ways $= 3 \times 2 = 6$ ways.

The correct answer is option B.

46. Since the question asks for calculating the number of ways of selecting, we will apply 'Combination' and not 'Permutation'.

We know that, number of ways of selecting r objects out of n objects $= C_r^n = \dfrac{n!}{r!\,(n-r)!}$

A = # of ways 11 players can be selected out of 25 players $= C_{11}^{25} = \dfrac{25!}{11!\,(14)!}$

B = # of ways 14 players can be selected out of 25 players $= C_{14}^{25} = \dfrac{25!}{14!\,(11)!}$

As we see that A and B are equal in value, there is no need to calculate the values.

The correct answer is option D.

47. For a 3-digit number to be even, its unit digit must be either 2 or 8.

Number of ways, unit place can be filled = 2 (either 2 or 8);

Number of ways, tens place can be filled = 4; it is given that the repetition of digits is allowed.

Number of ways, hundreds place can be filled = 4;

So, the total number of 3-digit even numbers = 2.4.4 = 32.

The correct answer is option C.

48. Number of ways, each letter can be chosen = 26
So, total number of ways of choosing 26 letters for three places = 26^3.

Similarly, number of ways, each digit can be chosen = 10
So, total number of ways of choosing 10 digits for three places = 10^3.

These two blocks of the digits and the letters can be arranged in 2 ways (At the beginning or at the end).

So, total number of ways = $2.26^3.10^3$ ways.

The correct answer is option D.

49. '3' can be placed in the following ways in 5-digit numbers: 3XXXX, X3XXX, XX3XX, XXX3X, and XXXX3. Since '3' has to appear only once, we have 9 choices for each vacant place out of digits 0-9 (excluding the digit '3').

But wait! A 5-digit number cannot begin with a digit '0', so the 5-digit numbers that do not begin with '3' will have only 8 number of ways to its fill ten-thousandth place.

For numbers X3XXX, XX3XX, XXX3X, and XXXX3, total number of ways = $4.8.9^3$

For number 3XXXX, total number of ways = 9^4

Hence, total number of ways = $9^4 + 4.8.9^3$

The correct answer is option D.

50. A triangle can be drawn taking any 3 vertices of a polygon.
So, the number of triangles = $C_3^8 = \dfrac{8.7.6}{1.2.3} = 56$

The correct answer is option C.

A regular Octagon (8-sided polygon) will not have 3 or more number of co-linear vertices, hence there is no need to think of deducting a few number of dummy triangles formed out of co-linear points.

What if the question had been:

How many triangles are possible out of 8 points lying in a plane, out of which 4 points are co-linear?

The answer would not be 56. There would be a few dummy triangles formed out of 4 co-linear points, and we must deduct those from 56.

Number of dummy triangles = $C_3^4 = C_1^4 = 4$

So, total number of genuine triangles = $56 - 4 = 52$ triangles

51. Since one specific individual must be in the team, the question becomes:

"How many ~~3~~ 2-member teams can be formed out of ~~6~~ 5 members?"

Number of ways of choosing 2 members from 5 individuals = $C_2^5 = \dfrac{5.4}{1.2} = 10$.

The correct answer is option B.

52. Number of ways of choosing only 2 boys out of 8 boys = $C_2^8 = \dfrac{8.7}{1.2} = 28$

Number of ways of choosing only 2 girls out of 10 girls = $C_2^{10} = \dfrac{10.9}{1.2} = 45$

Hence, the total number of ways = $28 + 45 = 73$; since this is a case of 'OR', we would add the number of ways.

The correct answer is option B.

53. We know that if there are total n objects, out of these there are p number of one type of identical objects, q number of another type of identical objects, and r number of another type of identical objects, then the number of ways these objects can be arranged in a row to have unique patterns = $\dfrac{n!}{p!.q!.r!}$

There are a total 6 letters in BANANA; so $n = 6$, and there are 3 As and 2 Ns, so $p = 3$, and $q = 2$.

Thus, the answer is $\dfrac{6!}{3!.2!} = 60$.

The correct answer is option B.

6.2   Student-Produced Response or Grid-In Questions

54.   For a 4-digit number to be even, its unit digit must be either 4 or 8.

Number of ways, unit place can be filled = 2 (either 4 or 8)

Number of ways, tenth place can be filled = 4; given that the repetition is allowed.

Number of ways, hundredth place can be filled = 4

Number of ways, thousandth place can be filled = 4

So, total number of ways = 2.4.4.4 = 128 ways.

1	2	8	

55.   A triangle can be drawn taking any 3 points on a plane.

So, the number of triangles = $C_3^9 = \dfrac{9.8.7}{1.2.3} = 84$

Since there are 3 co-linear points, so there would be a few dummy triangles formed out of three 3 collinear points, and we must deduct those from 84.

Number of dummy triangles = $C_3^3 = 1$ (This is in fact a straight line, passing through the 3 collinear points.)

So, total number of genuine triangles = 84 − 1 = 83

8	3		

56.   Number of ways of choosing 1 cube from Puzzle box1 = $C_1^{10} = 10$

Number of ways of choosing 2 cubes from Puzzle box2 = $C_2^5 = \dfrac{5.4}{1.2} = 10$

Total number of ways = 10.10 = 100

1	0	0	

57.   'Numbers between 1 and 9999, inclusive' means all 1-digit, 2-digit, 3-digit, and 4-digit numbers (1 to 9999).

Number of ways of making a 1-digit numbers out of the given 4 digits 0, 1, 2, and 3 = 3. "0" to be excluded)

Number of ways of making 2-digit numbers out of 4 digits 0, 1, 2, and 3 = 3.4 = 12 since the tenth place can be filled by 3 ways only (1, 2, or 3; a 2-digit number cannot begin with a '0'), whereas the unit place can be filled by 4 ways. (Remember that the repetition of digits is allowed. Questions does not restrict us to use the given digits only once.)

Similarly, the number of ways of making 3-digit numbers out of 4 digits 0, 1, 2, and 3 = 3.4.4 = 48.

Similarly, the number of ways of making 4-digit numbers out of 4 digits 0, 1, 2, and 3 = 3.4.4.4 = 192.

Total number of ways (Total 'between 1 and 9999, inclusive') = 3 + 12 + 48 + 192 = 255.

2	5	5	

58. Do read the question carefully. The question asks for the selection of 2 students and NOT '2 boys and 2 girls' OR '2 boys or 2 girls'.

So, the question is simply this: "In how many ways can 2 students be chosen from a class comprising 22 students (10 + 12)?" There is no need to specify how many boys and girls are in the class.

So, the number of ways of choosing 2 students out of 22 students $= C_2^{22} = \dfrac{22.21}{1.2} = 231$. The 231 selections include 1 boy and 1 girl, both boys, and both girls. The distribution of 22 students in 10 boys and 12 girls is given to confuse you. It is a superfluous information.

The correct answer is 231.

Note: Attempting the question in the following manner is wrong.

Number of ways of choosing 2 boys out of 10 boys $= C_2^{10} = \dfrac{10.9}{1.2} = 45$

Number of ways of choosing 2 girls out of 12 girls $= C_2^{12} = \dfrac{12.11}{1.2} = 66$

Or, the total number of ways (2 boys OR 2 girls) = 45 + 66 = 111 (Incorrect).

In other way, we deduce that there are 231 − 111 = 120 ways in which there would be 1 boy and 1 girl. Let's cross check this.

Number of ways of choosing 1 boy out of 10 boys = 10

Number of ways of choosing 1 girl out of 12 girls = 12

Or, the total number of ways (Selection of 2 students = 1 boy AND 1 girl) = 10.12 = 120. Since the keyword AND is applicable in this case, we have multiplied the number of ways.

2	3	1	

59. Number of ways n objects can be arranged in a circle $= (n-1)!$

So, the number of ways 6 cubes be arranged in a circle $= (6-1)! = 5! = 120$.

1	2	0	

60. We know that if there are total n objects, out of these there are p number of one type of identical objects, q number of another type of identical objects, and r number of another type of identical objects, then the number of ways these objects can be arranged in a row to have unique patterns $= \dfrac{n!}{p!.q!.r!}$

There are total 6 letters in "LETTER"; so $n = 6$, and there are 2 Es and 2 Ts, so $p = 2$, and $q = 2$.

Thus, the number of distinct words $= \dfrac{6!}{2!.2!} = \dfrac{6.5.4.3.2.1}{2.2} = 180$.

1	8	0	

61. An efficient approach to solve this question would be to club two "Es", compute the number of words, and then deduct those from the total number of possible words, we already calculated earlier without any restriction (180) in the previous question.

Considering two "Es" together, we now have a total 5 letters (L, E, T, T, R); so $n = 5$; since there are 2 Ts, $p = 2$. We will not take into account $q = 2$ as two "Es" are in fact one and not TWO!

Thus, the number of words with two "Es" together $= \dfrac{5!}{2!} = \dfrac{5.4.3.2.1}{2} = 60$.

Or, the number of words with NO two "Es" coming together $= 180 - 60 = 120$.

1	2	0	

62. Since the two tall students must NOT be included in the selection, the number of students left, out of which the 11 students must be selected $= 15 - 2 = 13$.

Number of ways 11 students of out 13 can be selected

$= C_{11}^{13} = C_{(13-11)}^{13} = C_2^{13} = \dfrac{13.12}{1.2} = 78$. **Note:** $C_r^n = C_{n-r}^n$

It is important to note that the arrangement of 11 students must be ignored as the order of selection does not matter.

7	8		

63.   A delegation of 5 generals can be done in any of the following ways:

      1) 1 general from UK (5), and 4 generals from France (6)
      2) 2 generals from UK (5), and 3 generals from France (6)
      3) 3 generals from UK (5), and 2 generals from France (6)

      Number of ways 1 general from 5 UK generals can be selected $= C_1^5 = \dfrac{5}{1} = 5$

      Number of ways 4 generals from 6 French generals can be selected $= C_4^6 = C_2^6 = \dfrac{6.5}{1.2} = 15$

      Total number of ways 1 general from UK (5), and 4 generals from France (6) can be selected = 5.15 = 75

      Similarly,

      Number of ways 2 generals from UK (5), and 3 generals from France (6) can be selected =
      $C_2^5 \times C_3^6 = \dfrac{5.4}{1.2} \times \dfrac{6.5.4}{1.2.3} = 200$

      Number of ways 3 generals from UK (5), and 2 generals from France (6) can be selected =
      $C_3^5 \times C_2^6 = \dfrac{5.4.3}{1.2.3} \times \dfrac{6.5}{1.2} = 150$

      Total number of ways = 75 + 200 + 150 = 425.

4	2	5	

64.   Say the captain is chosen, hence the number of players left to be chosen
      = 15 − 1 = 14.

      Again since the captain is already chosen, and the vice-captain & the injured player are not to be chosen, number of players left for selection = 18 − 1 − 2 = 15.

      Number of ways 14 players can be selected out of 15 players $= C_{14}^{15} = C_1^{15} = 15$. **Note:-** $C_r^n = C_{n-r}^n$

      If instead of the captain, the vice-captain is selected, again the number of ways = 15.
      Or, total number of ways = 2.15 = 30.

3	0		

65.   Since each of 6 members gifted each other, order or Permutation would be applicable as the father gifting a watch to his son is different than the son gifting a pen to his father.

      Since exchange of gift takes place between two, we must choose 2 members for exchanging gifts.

      Total number of gifts $= P_2^6 = 6.5 = 30$

The correct answer is 30.

Alternatively,

Each of 6 members will give 5 gift and receive 5 gifts; so total number of gifts = 6.5 = 30.

| 3 | 0 | | |

66. Unlike gifting each other, since a handshake between two people would be counted as a single handshake, order is not important; thus combination would be applicable.

Total number of handshakes = $C_2^6 = \dfrac{6.5}{1.2} = 15$

The correct answer is 15.

Alternatively,

Each of 6 members will shake hands 5 times, so total number of handshakes = (6.5)/2 = 30/2 = 15 (total number of handshakes must be halved as two handshakes would be counted as a single handshake.

| 1 | 5 | | |

67. There are a total of 5 symbols and we have to take all of them together to form codes, taking □ at the beginning of the codes. Let's fix the position of □, so we have to arrange only 4 symbols.

Number of ways 4 symbols can be arranged = $P_4^4 = 4! = 24$

| 2 | 4 | | |

68. The first possible password greater than 5999 would be 6012 and the last one would be 9876 as digits must NOT be repeated.

Lets us compute the number of ways total passwords can be generated.

Number of ways 1st place of 4-digit password can be filled = 4 (6, 7, 8, and 9)

Number of ways 2nd place of 4-digit password can be filled = 9 (Any digit from 0-9 except one digit among 6, 7, 8, and 9)

Number of ways 3rd place of 4-digit password can be filled = 8 (Any digit from 0-9 except the two digits used in 1st and 2nd places)

Number of ways 4th place of 4-digit password can be filled = 7 (Any digit from 0-9 except the three digits used in 1st, 2nd, and 3rd places)

Total number of passwords = 4.9.8.7 = 2016

2	0	1	6

69. Number of ways of choosing 2 boys out of 10 boys = $C_2^{10} = \dfrac{10.9}{1.2} = 45$

Number of ways of choosing 2 girls out of 12 girls = $C_2^{12} = \dfrac{12.11}{1.2} = 66$

Since this is a case of 'OR', we must add the number of ways, thus the answer is 66 + 45 = 111.

1	1	1	

70. We know that if there are total n objects, out of these there are p number of one type of identical objects, q number of another type of identical objects, and r number of another type of identical objects, then the number of ways these objects can be arranged in a row to have unique patterns = $\dfrac{n!}{p!.q!.r!}$

There are a total 6 letters in BANANA; there are 3 As and 2 Ns; since 2 'Ns' have to be together, let's consider them as one letter, thus, we have so $n = 6 - 1 = 5$, and $p = 3$.

Thus, the number of ways 2 'Ns' come together = $\dfrac{5!}{3!} = 20$.

But we are interested in finding out the number of ways 2 "Ns" do not come together.

Thus, the number of ways 2 'Ns' do not come together = total number of ways without any condition - the number of ways 2 'Ns' come together

Total number of ways without any condition = $\dfrac{6!}{3!.2!} = 60$.

Thus, the number of ways 2 'Ns' do not come together = 60 - 20 = 40.

4	0		

71. There are a total of 5 symbols and we have take all of them together to form codes, considering that the □ must NOT be at the beginning and the ◊ must NOT be at the end of the codes.

Number of ways 5 symbols can be arranged = $P_5^5 = 5! = 120$. We will deduct the number of codes which starts the □ with and ends with the ◊; thus this asks for the arrangement of 3 symbols.

Number of ways 3 symbols can be arranged = $P_3^3 = 3! = 6$.

Thus, the desired number of codes = $120 - 6 = 114$.

1	1	4	

Chapter 7

Probability

What are the chances of Messi winning the toss in a FIFA world cup match? Well, ideally it's 50%! He has an equal chance of winning and losing the toss, provided the coin and the trial are fair.

It is very important that the coin tossed is fair, else the coin will be called a biased coin, the outcomes of 'Head and Tail' would be influenced, and the chances of getting a Head and getting a Tail will not be 50-50.

What do we mean when we say that the chance of getting a Head is 50%?

It means that if we toss a coin many number of times, say 100 times, it is likely that the fair coin will fall Head 50 times and fall Tail 50 times. But can this occur practically? The answer is no. Just to share a fact that Carolina Panthers has lost 13 tosses consecutively; however it is so rare that it happens in 1 out of 8192 cases!

So, is there a significance of 50-50? Yes, there is. If, say, the experiment of throwing a fair coin is done over 100,000 times (Read: very large number of trials), it is very likely that you get Head close to 50,000 times.

7.1   Chance vs. Probability

Chance is a term used by common people; it is measured on a scale of '100'. The count of any event to occur out of 100 possibilities is a chance percent.

Probability is a term used by mathematicians; which is measured on a scale of '1' instead of '100'.

7.2   A few definitions

7.2.1   Experiment

Tossing a coin or throwing a die is an experiment. It is an activity that can be repeated infinite number of times and produces a well-defined set of outcomes. In an experiment, only one of all the possible outcomes is the result. Repetition of an experiment is called a **Trial**.

7.2.2   Event

In an experiment, getting a Head upon tossing a coin or getting a '3' on the upper face upon throwing a die is an event. Events are a set of all possible outcomes of an experiment. We may also talk about a favorable or an unfavorable event. Tossing a coin renders two events: {Head and Tail}, while throwing a die renders six events: {1, 2, 3, 4, 5, 6}. In an experiment with a die, if you were to have '5' as an outcome, then getting a '5' is a favorable event, and not getting a '5' are unfavorable events.

7.2.3   Equally likely events

If the chances of occurrence of some events are equal, they are called equally likely events. For a fair die, the chance of the occurrence of '3' equals that of '5'. So, these events are equally likely. Similarly, for a coin, the chance of getting a 'Head' equals that of a 'Tail'.

7.2.4   Sample set

A set of all possible outcomes of an experiment is called the sample set. For a fair die, the sample set is {1, 2, 3, 4, 5, 6}; whereas for a coin, the sample set is {Head, Tail}.

$$\text{Probability of an event} = \frac{\text{Number of favorable events}}{\text{Total number of events}}$$

Question: What is the probability of getting an outcome as Head in an experiment of tossing a fair coin?

The sample set is {Head, Tail}, so only two events are possible; out of these two events, only one event—Head is the favorable event.

$$\text{P(Head)} = \frac{\text{Number of favorable events}}{\text{Total number of events}} = \frac{n(\text{favorable events})}{n(\text{total events})} = \frac{1}{2}$$

Question: In an experiment of throwing a die, what is the probability of getting an outcome as '2' or '4' on the upper face of an unbiased die?

The sample set is {1, 2, 3, 4, 5, 6}, so there are a total six events; out of these six events, two events: {2, 4} are the favorable events.

$$\text{Probability of '2' or '4'} = \frac{n(\text{favorable events})}{n(\text{total events})} = \frac{n\{2,4\}}{n\{1,2,3,4,5,6\}} = \frac{2}{6} = \frac{1}{3}$$

Sum of probabilities of all events = '1'. Event with probability = 1 is called a **Certain event.**

$$\text{P(H or T)} = \frac{n(\text{favorable events})}{n(\text{total events})} = \frac{2}{2} = 1$$

Probability cannot be less than '0'. Event with probability = 0 is called an **Impossible event.**

$$\text{Probability (neither Head nor Tail)} = \frac{n(\text{favorable events})}{n(\text{total events})} = \frac{0}{2} = 0$$

So, we can deduce that:

$$\boxed{0 \le P(A) \le 1}$$

Question: There are 2 red, 4 green, and 5 black balls in a bag. If a ball is drawn randomly, what is the probability that it is a green color ball?

$$\text{P(G)} = \frac{n(\text{ favorable events})}{n(\text{total events})} = \frac{4}{(2+4+5)} = \frac{4}{11}$$

7.3   An experiment with two dice

 Die is singular and **Dice** is plural. Two dice will have $6 \times 6 = 36$ sample points or possible events. The sample set of SUM would be $\{2, 3, 4, 5, 6, 7, 8, 9, 10, 11, 12\}$; each element in the set is the sum of outcomes on the upper face of each die.

Let us list down the number ways each sum can be formed.

Sum	Ways	Number of ways	Frequency distribution & Probabilities
2	{1,1}	1	$p = \dfrac{1}{36}$
3	{2,1}, {1,2}	2	$p = \dfrac{1}{18}$
4	{3,1}, {2,2}, {1,3}	3	$p = \dfrac{1}{12}$
5	{4,1}, {3,2}, {2,3}, {1,4}	4	$p = \dfrac{1}{9}$
6	{5,1}, {4,2}, {3,3}, {2,4}, {1,5}	5	$p = \dfrac{5}{36}$
7	{6,1}, {5,2}, {4,3}, {3,4}, {2,5}, {1,6}	6	$p = \dfrac{1}{6}$
8	{6,2}, {5,3}, {4,4}, {3,5}, {2,6}	5	$p = \dfrac{5}{36}$
9	{6,3}, {5,4}, {4,5}, {3,6}	4	$p = \dfrac{1}{9}$
10	{6,4}, {5,5}, {4,6}	3	$p = \dfrac{1}{12}$
11	{6,5}, {5,6}	2	$p = \dfrac{1}{18}$
12	{6,6}	1	$p = \dfrac{1}{36}$
	Total number of ways	36	

Memorise...

1. **If Sum ≤ 7, then Number of ways = Sum – 1**

2. **If Sum ≥ 8, then Number of ways = 13 – Sum**

Question: What is the probability of getting a sum of '5' on the upper faces of two unbiased dice?

The sample set is $\{2, 3, 4, 5, 6, 7, 8, 9, 10, 11, 12\}$; and there are a total 36 possible events.

Probability of getting a total of '5' on the upper faces of dice

$= \dfrac{n(\text{favorable events})}{n(\text{total events})} = \dfrac{4}{36} = \dfrac{1}{9}$

7.4   A few more definitions

7.4.1   Mutually Exclusive Events

If two events cannot occur together, they are called **Mutually Exclusive** events or **Disjoint** events.

Example: Getting a Head and a Tail on the upper face of a coin; another example, getting a '3' and a '5' in a throw of a die.

> Since for a coin, only one of the two events—Head or Tail will occur at a time, hence they are mutually exclusive events; similarly, if '3' appears on the upper face of the die, it is obvious that '5' will not appear.

Following Venn diagram represents the scenario.

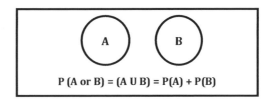

However, an event of getting '3' and 'prime number' in a throw of a die is not mutually exclusive as '3' is an element of the set of prime numbers.

If the events are joint or non-mutually exclusive, then the following formula applies.

P(A or B) = P(A $\cup$ B) = P(A) + P(B) – P(A & B)

Following Venn diagram represents the scenario.

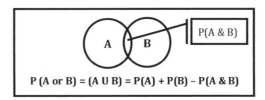

The table below depicts the difference between mutually exclusive and joint events with an application of an example.

Event	Example	Solution
Disjoint (Mutually exclusive)	A die is rolled. What is the probability of getting a '3' or a '5' on the upper face of the die?	P('3') = 1/6; P('5') = 1/6; So, P('3' or '5') = (1/6) + (1/6) = 1/3.
Joint	A die is rolled. What is the probability of getting a '3' or a 'Prime number' on the upper face of the die?	P('3') = 1/6; P('Prime') = 3/6 = 1/2; P('3' & 'P') = 1/6 ('3' is common in Prime numbers: 2, 3, and 5); So, P('3' or 'P') = (1/6) + (1/2) – (1/6) = 1/2.

7.4.2 Independent Events

Two events are called independent if the occurrence of one event does not affect the occurrence of the other.

Example: In a throw of two dice, the occurrence of a '3' on the first die does not influence the occurrence of any number on the second die; hence these events are independent events.

For independent events, **P(A & B) = P(A $\cap$ B) = P(A) $\times$ P(B)**

If the events are not independent, then the concept of 'conditional probability' is involved; however this concept is not frequently tested on the SAT.

7.4.3 Exhaustive event

A set of events is called **Exhaustive** if there is no possibility of any other event to occur other than the events in the set; in other words, one of those events must occur. For example: In the toss of a coin, Events of a Head and a Tail are exhaustive events. (assuming, of course, that the coin does not land on its side!)

7.5   AND vs. OR rule

In a nut shell, you must know rules for probability calculations on the SAT: "AND" means MULTIPLY, and "OR" means ADDITION.

Concept	Application	Example	Solution
AND	×; multiply the probabilities	A coin is tossed twice. What is the probability of getting a Head in first trial, and Tail in the second trial?	P(Head in I trial) = 1/2; P(Tail in II trial) = 1/2; So, P(HT) = (1/2) × (1/2) = 1/4.
OR	+; add the probabilities	A die is rolled. What is the probability of getting a '3' **or** an 'Even number' on the upper face of the die?	P('3') = 1/6; P('E') = 3/6 = 1/2; So, P('3' or 'E') = (1/6) + (1/2) = 2/3.

7.6   Conditional Probability

The concept of conditional probability relates to deducing the probability of an event given that another event has already occurred. This concept is important since the occurrence of one event can affect the probability of a dependent event.

The conditional probability of A given B is denoted by $P(A|B)$, it means probability of A if event B has occurred.

$$P(A|B) = \frac{P(A \cap B)}{P(B)}$$

Question: What is the probability of getting a '3' on the upper face of a die given that the number appeared is a 'Prime number'?

Say, P('3') = probability of getting a '3';
and P('P') = probability of getting a 'Prime number'

We know that P('P') = 1/2;
and P('3'∩'P') = 1/6

So, $P(3|P) = \dfrac{P(3 \cap P)}{P(P)} = \dfrac{1/6}{1/2} = 1/3$

Logical deduction approach:

Since there are only three prime numbers: 2, 3, & 5 and '3' is one of them, hence the chance of getting '3' out of '2', '3' and '5' is 33.33% = 1/3.

7.7   Independent and Dependent Events

- For **Independent Events: P(A|B) = P(A)**;

- For **Dependent Events: P(A|B) ≠ P(A)**

Question: A bag contains 3 yellow and 7 blue marbles. What is the probability of drawing a yellow marble in the first draw and then drawing a blue marble in the second draw?

Let us understand the concept of dependent event.

The second event–drawing a blue marble–is a dependent event since the draw of a yellow marble in the first draw will increase the probability of drawing a blue marble in the second draw; while the draw of a blue marble in the first draw will decrease the probability of drawing another blue marble in the second draw. So the second event is a dependent event.

Let us see how.

(1) If a yellow marble is drawn in the first draw, then the bag will contain $\cancel{3}2$ yellow and 7 blue marbles; this makes the probability of drawing the blue marble in the second draw equals to 7/(2 + 7) = 7/9.

(2) If a blue marble is drawn in the first draw, then the bag will contain 3 yellow and $\cancel{7}6$ blue marbles; this makes the probability of drawing the blue marble in the second draw equals to 6/(3 + 6) = 6/9 = 2/3.

Clearly, 7/9 ≠ 2/3 implies that the probability of the second event is dependent on that of the first event.

Coming back to the question...

Drawing a yellow marble in the first draw = 3/10.
Drawing a blue marble in the second draw = 7/9.

So, the probability of drawing a yellow marble in the first draw, and blue marble in the second draw = (3/10) × (7/9) = 7/30.

7.8   Complement of an Event

If the occurrence of an event is denoted as A, then its non-occurrence is denoted as A' or A^C.

=> **Probability of occurrence an event + Probability of non-occurrence an event = 1.**

So, $P(A')$ or $P(A^C) = 1 - P(A)$;

or $P(A) + P(A') = 1$

Question: If a coin is tossed 3 times, what is the probability that it lands up on heads at least once?

Traditional approach:

P (Head ≥ 1) = P (Head = 1; Tail = 2) + P (Head = 2; Tail = 1) + P (Head = 3; Tail = none);

=> (Head = 1; Tail = 2) can occur in 3 ways; HTT, THT, and TTH;

   For each way, P (Head = 1; Tail = 2) = (1/2) × (1/2 × 1/2) = 1/8;

   So, for all 3 ways, P (Head = 1; Tail = 2) = 3 × (1/8) = 3/8.

=> Similarly, (Head = 2; Tail = 1) can occur in 3 ways; HHT, THH, and HTH;

   Again, for each way, P (Head = 2; Tail = 1) = (1/2) × (1/2 × 1/2) = 1/8;

   So, for all 3 ways, P (Head = 2; Tail = 1) = 3 × (1/8) = 3/8.

=> At last, (Head = 3; Tail = none) can occur in only one way; HHH;

   P (Head = 3; Tail = none) = (1/2 × 1/2 × 1/2) = 1/8.

So, P (Head ≥ 1) = P (Head = 1; Tail = 2) + P (Head = 2; Tail = 1) + P (Head = 3; Tail = none);
$$= 3/8 + 3/8 + 1/8$$
$$= 7/8.$$
This approach is time consuming. Let us see an alternate approach.

Alternate approach:

P (Head ≥ 1) = 1 − P (Head < 1)' = 1 − P (Head = 0; Tail = 3)
$$= 1 − (1/2 × 1/2 × 1/2)$$
$$= 7/8.$$

So, the learning is that we can make use of the concept of complement of an event to shorten the calculations.

7.9   Application of combination

What if the question is like the following?

Question: If a coin is tossed 3 times, what is the probability that it lands up on Head at least twice?

   In this question, the alternate approach and the traditional approach will take almost the same time.

Alternate approach:

P (Head ≥ 2) = 1 − P (Head < 2)′ = 1 − P (Head = 0; Tail = 3) − P (Head = 1; Tail = 2)

You will have to do the calculations twice–once for P (Head = 0; Tail = 3), and then for P (Head = 1; Tail = 2).

Traditional approach:

P (Head ≥ 2) = P (Head = 2; Tail = 1) + P (Head = 3; Tail = none)

Again, you will have to do the calculations twice–once for P (Head = 2; Tail = 1), and then for P (Head = 3; Tail = none). Practically there is no saving of time!

However, with the application of the concept of combination, we can save some time.

Let us take a seemingly time-consuming question.

Question: If a coin is tossed 5 times, what is the probability that it lands up on Head at least thrice?

P (Head ≥ 3) = P (Head = 3; Tail = 2) + P (Head = 4; Tail = 1) + P (Head = 5; Tail = none)

The meaning of (Head = 3; Tail = 2) is that we want 3 Heads occurring in 3 out of 5 trials, so it can be deduced that we want to choose 3 events out of 5 events, which is equal to C_3^5.

So, P (Head = 3; Tail = 2) = $C_3^5 \times [(1/2 \times 1/2 \times 1/2) \times (1/2 \times 1/2)]$
= $C_2^5 \times (1/2)^5 = (5.4)/(1.2) \times (1/2)^5 = (5.4)/(1.2) \times (1/2)^5 = 5/2^4$.
(Note that $C_3^5 = C_2^5$)

Similarly, P (Head = 4; Tail = 1) = $C_4^5 \times [(1/2 \times 1/2 \times 1/2 \times 1/2) \times (1/2)]$
= $C_1^5 \times (1/2)^5 = 5/2^5$.

And, P (Head = 5; Tail = none) = $C_5^5 \times (1/2 \times 1/2 \times 1/2 \times 1/2 \times 1/2) = 1 \times (1/2)^5$
= 2^5.

So, P (Head ≥ 3) = $5/2^4 + 5/2^5 + 1/2^5 = 16/2^5 = 1/2$.

P (Head ≥ 3) = 1/2.

Let us see one more question.

Question: A bag contains 4 yellow and 5 blue marbles. If three marbles are drawn simultaneously, what is the probability of drawing a yellow and two blue marbles?

P(Y = 1; B = 2)

$$= \frac{(\text{\# of ways one yellow marble can be drawn}) \times (\text{\# of ways two blue marbles can be drawn})}{(\text{\# of ways three marbles can be drawn})}$$

$$= \frac{(C_1^4).(C_2^5)}{C_3^9} = 4 \times \left[\frac{\dfrac{5.4}{1.2}}{\dfrac{9.8.7}{1.2.3}} \right] = \frac{10}{21}.$$

Now we see exam-like questions in the next chapter.

Chapter 8

Practice Questions

Probability is a part of **Problem Solving and Data Analysis** of the revised SAT. You will have calculator access for all the questions.

8.1 Multiple Choice Questions

1. A box contains 30 balls, of which 10 are black, 10 are green, and 10 are yellow. If two balls are drawn from the box at random, what is the probability that both the balls will be green?

    (A) 3/29

    (B) 1/9

    (C) 1/3

    (D) 2/3

    Solve yourself:

2. An unbiased coin is tossed thrice. What is the probability of getting at least one Head?

    (A) 1/8

    (B) 3/8

    (C) 1/2

    (D) 7/8

    Solve yourself:

3. A class of 36 students has an equal number of boys and girls. Four students are randomly selected to form a cultural committee. If the first three selected students are boys, what is the probability that the 4th student is also a boy?

    (A) 1/33

    (B) 1/15

    (C) 5/12

    (D) 5/11

Solve yourself:

4. A delegation of 9 diplomats comprises 3 Japanese and 6 Chinese. If 3 diplomats are to be chosen at random from the delegation, what is the probability that at least 2 diplomats are Japanese?

   (A) 1/12

   (B) 3/14

   (C) 19/84

   (D) 1/3

   Solve yourself:

5. John, Peter, and Harry are given an assignment to collectively solve a problem. The probabilities of John, Peter and Harry to solve the problem individually are 4/5, 2/3, and 3/4 respectively. What is the probability that the problem will not be solved?

   (A) 1/60

   (B) 13/60

   (C) 2/3

   (D) 47/60

   Solve yourself:

6. John and Harry are among the 5 promising soccer players in the school. 3 out of 5 players are to be chosen at random. What is the probability that both John and Harry would be chosen?

   (A) 1/10

   (B) 1/5

   (C) 3/10

   (D) 2/5

Solve yourself:

7. Three actors are to be chosen out of five — Jack, Steve, Elad, Suzy, and Ali. What is the probability that Jack and Steve would be chosen, but Suzy would be left out?

    (A) 1/5

    (B) 2/5

    (C) 3/5

    (D) 7/10

    Solve yourself:

8. A box contains p number of silver coins and q number of gold coins. One coin is randomly drawn from the box but not replaced; thereafter a second coin is randomly drawn. What is the probability that the first coin drawn is silver and the second is gold?

    (A) $\left(\dfrac{p}{p+q}\right)\left(\dfrac{q}{p+q}\right)$

    (B) $\left(\dfrac{p}{p+q}\right)\left(\dfrac{p-1}{p+q-1}\right)$

    (C) $\left(\dfrac{p-1}{p+q}\right)\left(\dfrac{q-1}{p+q}\right)$

    (D) $\left(\dfrac{p}{p+q}\right)\left(\dfrac{q}{p+q-1}\right)$

    Solve yourself:

9. A super mall issues coupons to its customers at the entrance of the mall. The coupons are numbered from 100 to 400, inclusive. Customers who have coupons with the numbers divisible by '2' will win gifts. What is the probability that a random customer wins a gift?

(A) 149/300
(B) 150/301
(C) 151/301
(D) 1/2

Solve yourself:

10. There are 2 groups — Group A comprises of only 50 married men, while group B comprises of only 40 married women. Between these groups, there are only 5 husband-wife pairs. If one man and one woman is randomly chosen from each group, what is the probability that they make a husband-wife pair?

(A) 1/400
(B) 1/80
(C) 1/18
(D) 1/9

Solve yourself:

11. A box contains 30 balls, of which 10 are black, 10 are green, and 10 are yellow balls. If two balls are drawn from the box at random one after the other (with replacement), what is the probability that both the balls will be green?

(A) 3/29
(B) 1/9
(C) 1/4
(D) 1/3

Solve yourself:

12. A box contains 4 black and few green balls. If two balls are drawn from the box at random, and the probability that both the balls are black is 1/6, how many green balls are in the box?

(A) 3

(B) 4

(C) 5

(D) 6

Solve yourself:

13. In an aptitude examination, there are 41 questions with 5 options. A candidate knows the correct answers of 16 questions, unsure between 2 options for 10 questions, unsure among 3 options for 6 questions, unsure among 4 options for 4 questions, and unsure among all 5 options for 5 questions. How many questions can he probably mark correct?

(A) 24

(B) 25

(C) 26

(D) 27

Solve yourself:

14. A tool-box contains 10 spanners, out of which 3 are defective. If a mechanic randomly selects 2 spanners at a time, what is the probability that at least one spanner will be defective?

(A) 2/9

(B) 3/10

(C) 7/15

(D) 8/15

Solve yourself:

15. A class comprises of 20 students, out of which 15 are boys and the rest are girls. If a committee of 3 students is to be formed, what is the probability that there would be only one boy in the committee?

(A) 5/38

(B) 3/10

(C) 35/76

(D) 41/76

Solve yourself:

16. The probability that a man can shoot and hit a target is 1/100. If the man fires 100 rounds, what is the probability that all the 100 shots do not miss the target?

(A) $\left(\dfrac{1}{10}\right)^{200}$

(B) $\dfrac{10^{200} - 1}{10^{200}}$

(C) $\left(\dfrac{1}{100}\right)^2$

(D) $\dfrac{(100^{100} - 99^{100})}{100^{100}}$

Solve yourself:

17. A group of 12 people comprises 3 Japanese, 4 Australians, and 5 Chinese. If 4 people are to be chosen at random from the group to form a committee, what is the probability that 2 members are Japanese?

(A) 3/55

(B) 12/55

(C) 3/11

(D) 49/55

Solve yourself:

18. A gambler bets everyday on soccer games. If the probability of him loosing the bet each day is 0.4, what is the probability that he wins on only 2 days out of 3 days he bets?

    (A) 0.144

    (B) 0.16

    (C) 0.36

    (D) 0.432

    Solve yourself:

19.

A box has 10 cards, each written with a different digit on it, from 0-9. Four cards cards shown above were drawn from it. What is the probability of picking two cards written with odd integers on them from the remaining cards in the box?

    (A) 1/4

    (B) 1/5

    (C) 1/6

    (D) 1/7

    Solve yourself:

20. An integer is randomly picked from the set $\{-6, -4, -2, 0, 2, 4, 6\}$; what is the probability that the the the integer satisfies the inequality $|2x - 3| > 3$?

    (A) 2/7

    (B) 3/7

    (C) 4/7

    (D) 5/7

Solve yourself:

21. Probability that a missile will hit its target is 0.6. If three missiles are fired at the target, what is the probability of hitting the target at least once?

    (A) 0.096

    (B) 0.6

    (C) 0.936

    (D) 0.964

    Solve yourself:

22. What is the probability of randomly selecting two numbers simultaneously from numbers 1 to 100 (both inclusive) so that the two numbers are odd perfect squares?

    (A) $\dfrac{1}{990}$

    (B) $\dfrac{1}{495}$

    (C) $\dfrac{1}{20}$

    (D) $\dfrac{1}{10}$

    Solve yourself:

23. What is the probability of randomly selecting two numbers simultaneously from numbers 1 to 50 (both inclusive) so that the two numbers are neither prime nor perfect squares?

    (A) 0.50

    (B) 0.40

    (C) 0.31

(D)   0.21

Solve yourself:

24.   Three balls are drawn successively without repetition from a bag containing four white, three red and three blue balls. What is the probability that the three balls are of different colors?

  (A) $\dfrac{3}{10}$

  (B) $\dfrac{1}{5}$

  (C) $\dfrac{2}{9}$

  (D) $\dfrac{5}{21}$

  Solve yourself:

25.   There are two bags, one contains three white and two black balls, while the other contains four white and five black balls. What is the probability that if one ball is drawn from each bag, they will be of the same color?

  (A) $\dfrac{11}{45}$

  (B) $\dfrac{22}{45}$

  (C) $\dfrac{1}{2}$

  (D) $\dfrac{3}{4}$

  Solve yourself:

26. A box contains three blue and two red balls, while another box contains four green and two white balls. A coin is tossed. If 'heads' appears, a ball is drawn from the first box and if a tail appears, a ball is drawn from the second box. What is the probability of drawing a blue ball?

    (A) 0.1

    (B) 0.2

    (C) 0.3

    (D) 0.6

    Solve yourself:

27. If for a biased die, the probability of appearance of an even number is double that of an odd number, what is the probability of consecutive 6s appearing on two throws of the die?

    (A) $\dfrac{1}{36}$

    (B) $\dfrac{2}{9}$

    (C) $\dfrac{4}{81}$

    (D) $\dfrac{5}{81}$

    Solve yourself:

28. Three balls are simultaneously drawn from a box containing five yellow and four green balls. What is the probability that the three balls are not all of the same color?

    (A) 0.167

    (B) 0.33

    (C) 0.83

    (D) 0.89

    Solve yourself:

29. Given that

   • A = Probability of drawing two red balls from a bag containing 12 red and 10 blue balls

   • B = Probability of drawing two blue balls from a bag containing 12 red and 10 blue balls

   • C = Probability of drawing one red and one blue ball from a bag containing 12 red and 10 blue balls

   Which of the following statement is correct?

   (A) $A < B < C$

   (B) $A > C > B$

   (C) $A > B > C$

   (D) $C > A > B$

   Solve yourself:

30. Four friends A, B, C and D stand in a line for a photograph. What is the probability that A stands to the immediate left of C?

   (A) $\dfrac{1}{6}$

   (B) $\dfrac{1}{4}$

   (C) $\dfrac{1}{3}$

   (D) $\dfrac{1}{2}$

   Solve yourself:

31. A bag has 20 blue and 10 red balls. What is the probability of drawing two balls simultaneously so that they are not of the same color?

   (A) 0.13

   (B) 0.26

   (C) 0.36

(D) 0.46

Solve yourself:

32. What is the probability of selecting x from the set $\{-2, 0, 2, 4, 6\}$ such that $x^2 \leq 16$?

   (A) $\dfrac{1}{5}$

   (B) $\dfrac{2}{5}$

   (C) $\dfrac{3}{5}$

   (D) $\dfrac{4}{5}$

   Solve yourself:

33. What is the probability of obtaining the same number on each throw if a die is thrown thrice?

   (A) $\dfrac{1}{36}$

   (B) $\dfrac{1}{3}$

   (C) $\dfrac{1}{2}$

   (D) $\dfrac{2}{3}$

   Solve yourself:

34. What is the probability of obtaining an odd number or a prime number on one throw of a dice?

   (A) $\dfrac{1}{6}$

(B) $\dfrac{1}{3}$

(C) $\dfrac{2}{3}$

(D) $\dfrac{3}{4}$

Solve yourself:

35. What is the probability of getting a number on the first throw greater than that on the second throw when a dice is thrown twice?

(A) $\dfrac{1}{6}$

(B) $\dfrac{5}{12}$

(C) $\dfrac{7}{12}$

(D) $\dfrac{2}{3}$

Solve yourself:

36. What is the probability of selecting two cards successively with replacement from five cards numbered '1' to '5' so that the sum of the numbers is '8'?

(A) $\dfrac{3}{25}$

(B) $\dfrac{2}{5}$

(C) $\dfrac{3}{5}$

(D) $\dfrac{4}{5}$

Solve yourself:

37. What is the probability of obtaining '3' at least once on throwing a dice twice?

    (A) $\dfrac{5}{18}$

    (B) $\dfrac{11}{36}$

    (C) $\dfrac{7}{18}$

    (D) $\dfrac{25}{36}$

Solve yourself:

38. What is the probability of choosing a number from the set such that the selected number is the mean of the set: {1, 2, 2, 3, 4, 5, 5, 5, 9}?

    (A) $\dfrac{1}{10}$

    (B) $\dfrac{1}{9}$

    (C) $\dfrac{1}{8}$

    (D) $\dfrac{2}{9}$

Solve yourself:

39. What is the probability of selecting two numbers, one from set A: {1, 3, 6} and the other from B: {2, 3, 8} so that the sum of the numbers is 9?

    (A) $\dfrac{2}{9}$

    (B) $\dfrac{1}{9}$

    (C) $\dfrac{1}{10}$

    (D) $\dfrac{1}{12}$

Solve yourself:

40. What is the probability of selecting two numbers, one from set A: {1, 3, 6} and the other from B: {2, 3, 8} so that the product of the numbers is 9?

(A) $\dfrac{2}{9}$

(B) $\dfrac{1}{9}$

(C) $\dfrac{1}{10}$

(D) $\dfrac{1}{12}$

Solve yourself:

41. How many red balls are there in a bag that contains 24 balls of red, blue and green colors; given that the probability of drawing a blue ball is $\dfrac{1}{4}$ and the probability of drawing a green ball is $\dfrac{2}{3}$?

(A) One

(B) Two

(C) Three

(D) Four

Solve yourself:

42. Given that

    • A = Probability of getting all heads when three coins are tossed

    • B = Probability of getting all tails when three coins are tossed

    • C = Probability of getting two heads and one tail when three coins are tossed

    Which of the following statement is correct?

    (A) $A = 3B = 6C$

    (B) $A = C = 3B$

    (C) $A = B = C$

    (D) $C = 3A = 3B$

    Solve yourself:

43. A box contains 30 balls, of which 10 are black, 10 are green, and 10 are yellow. If two balls are drawn from the box at random, what is the probability that both the balls will be green?

    (A) 3/29

    (B) 1/9

    (C) 1/3

    (D) 2/3

    Solve yourself:

44. An unbiased coin is tossed thrice. What is the probability of getting at least one Head?

    (A) 1/8

    (B) 3/8

    (C) 1/2

    (D) 7/8

Solve yourself:

45. John, Peter, and Harry are given an assignment to collectively solve a problem. The probabilities of John, Peter and Harry to solve the problem individually are 4/5, 2/3, and 3/4 respectively. What is the probability that the problem will not be solved?

(A) 1/60

(B) 13/60

(C) 2/3

(D) 47/60

Solve yourself:

46. Three actors are to be chosen out of five — Jack, Steve, Elad, Suzy, and Ali. What is the probability that Jack and Steve would be chosen, but Suzy would be left out?

(A) 1/5

(B) 2/5

(C) 3/5

(D) 7/10

Solve yourself:

47. A box contains p number of silver coins and q number of gold coins. One coin is randomly drawn from the box but not replaced; thereafter a second coin is randomly drawn. What is the probability that both the coins are silver?

(A) $\dfrac{pq}{(p+q)^2}$

(B) $\dfrac{p(p-1)}{(p+q)(p+q-1)}$

(C) $\dfrac{(p-1)(q-1)}{(p+q)^2}$

(D) $\dfrac{pq}{(p+q)(p+q-1)}$

Solve yourself:

48. A super mall issues coupons to its customers at the entrance of the mall. The coupons are numbered from 100 to 400, inclusive. Customers who have coupons with the numbers divisible by '2' will win gifts. What is the probability that a random customer wins a gift?

(A)   149/300

(B)   150/301

(C)   151/301

(D)   1/2

Solve yourself:

49. A box contains 4 black and few green balls. If two balls are drawn from the box at random, and the probability that both the balls are black is 1/6, how many green balls are in the box?

(A)   3

(B)   4

(C)   5

(D)   6

Solve yourself:

50.

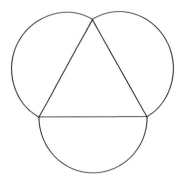

Above figure shows a designer dartboard. It has a triangle at the center with side 4 cm. Each side of the triangle is the diameter of the respective semi-circle. If Brian throws a dart, and it hits the dartboard, what is the probability that it hits triangular part of the dartboard?

(A) 1/2

(B) 1/4

(C) $\dfrac{2\sqrt{3}}{2\sqrt{3} + 6\pi}$

(D) $\dfrac{4\sqrt{3}}{4\sqrt{3} + 6\pi}$

Solve yourself:

8.2 Student-Produced Response or Grid-In Questions

51. A coin is tossed 6 times. What is the probability of getting exactly five Tails and one Head?

Solve yourself:

52. A pair of die is rolled. What is the probability of getting a sum of numbers on their upper faces greater than 9?

Solve yourself:

53. A die is rolled three times. What is the probability of getting a number greater than '2' for the first time, greater than '3' for the second time, and greater than '4' for the third time?

Solve yourself:

54. If the probability of Aleck watching the NBA final is 1/4, that of Ben is 1/3, and the probability of Chris NOT watching it is 1/2, what is the probability that Aleck and Chris will watch the NBA final but Ben will not?

Solve yourself:

55. Two students are chosen from a class comprising 10 boys and 10 girls. What is the probability that both would be boys?

Solve yourself:

56. Two students are chosen from a class comprising 10 boys and 12 girls. What is the probability that both would be either boys or girls?

Solve yourself:

57. In a school, there are 120 students. 68 play Soccer, and 48 play Basketball, while 30 play neither. If a student is randomly picked from the school, what is the probability that the student plays ONLY Soccer?

Solve yourself:

58. In the above question, what is the probability of picking a student who plays ONLY soccer given that he plays Soccer?

Solve yourself:

Following two questions are based on the table.

Employees during the year 2014-2015			
Employees	Permanent	Temporary	Total
Male	80	30	110
Female	30	40	70
Total	110	70	180

59. Based on the table above, what is the probability that an employee is male given that he/she is a permanent employee?

Solve yourself:

60. Based on the table above, if the company wishes to increase the headcount of female employees to 105 in the year 2015-16, keeping the same proportion of permanent female to temporary female employees, what is the expected number of permanent female employees in the company?

Solve yourself:

61.

Above figure shows a dartboard. Radius of the the outermost circle is three times the radius of the inner circle, and the radius of the middle circle is two times the radius of the inner circle. If Brian throws a dart, and it hits the dartboard, what is the probability that it hits the gray part of the dartboard?

Solve yourself:

62. A tool-box contains 10 spanners, out of which x are defective. If a mechanic randomly selects two spanners at a time, and the probability that both the selected spanners are defective is 2/15, what is the value of x?

Solve yourself:

63. In an urn, there are red, yellow, and green balls. If the ratio of number of red balls to number of yellow balls is 47 : 37, and the ratio of number of yellow balls to number of green balls is 148 : 67, what is the probability that a ball chosen randomly from the urn is a green ball?

Solve yourself:

64. If $x + y = 5$, and one of x and y is a non-negative integer, while the other is a positive integer less than 5. What is the probability that $x \geq 1$?

Solve yourself:

65. A coin is tossed three times. What is the probability that one gets Heads on the first two tosses and Tail on the third toss?

Solve yourself:

66. A pair of die is rolled. What is the probability of getting the sum of numbers greater than 10 on their upper faces?

Solve yourself:

67. A coin is tossed three times. What is the probability that one gets Heads on the first two tosses and Tail on the third toss?

| | | | |

Solve yourself:

68. A die is rolled three times. What is the probability of getting a number greater than '2' for the first time, greater than '3' for the second time, and greater than '4' for the third time?

| | | | |

Solve yourself:

69. A die is rolled four times. What is the probability of getting a number greater than '2' in the first time, greater than '3' in the second time, greater than '4' in the third time, and greater than '5' in the fourth time?

| | | | |

Solve yourself:

Chapter 9

Answer Key

9.1 Multiple Choice Questions

(1) A

(2) D

(3) D

(4) C

(5) A

(6) C

(7) A

(8) D

(9) C

(10) A

(11) B

(12) C

(13) B

(14) D

(15) A

(16) D

(17) B

(18) D

(19) B

(20) D

(21) C

(22) B

(23) C

(24) A

(25) B

(26) C

(27) C

(28) C

(29) D

(30) B

(31) D

(32) D

(33) A

(34) C

(35) B

(36) A

(37) C

(38) C

(39) B

(40) C

(41) B

(42) D

(43) A

(44) D

(45) A

(46) A

(47) B

(48) C

(49) C

(50) D

9.2   Student-Produced Response or Grid-In Questions

(51) 3/32

(52) 1/6

(53) 1/9

(54) 1/12

(55) 9/38

(56) 0.48

(57) 7/20

(58) 0.62

(59) 8/11

(60) 45

(61) 1/3

(62) 4

(63) 0.17

(64) 1

(65) 1/8

(66) 1/12

(67) 1/8

(68) 1/9

(69) 1/54

Chapter 10

Solutions

Probability is a part of **Problem Solving and Data Analysis** of the revised SAT. You will have calculator access for all the questions.

10.1 Multiple Choice Questions

1. Probability of an event $= \dfrac{\text{Number of favorable events}}{\text{Number of total events}}$;

   Here, number of favorable events = number of ways 2 green balls can be selected from 10 balls $= C_2^{10}$;

   Number of total events = number of ways 2 balls can be selected from 30 balls $= C_2^{30}$

   Hence, probability of getting both the green balls $= \dfrac{C_2^{10}}{C_2^{30}} = \dfrac{10.9/1.2}{30.29/1.2} = \dfrac{3}{29}$

   The correct answer is option A.

2. Since the coin is unbiased, it means that probabilities of getting a 'Head' or getting a 'Tail' upon a single toss are equal = 1/2.

   Traditional approach of solving this question would be to find the probability for each time the coin turns Head and then add them, but that is a lengthy process.

   An efficient approach would be to find out the probability of not getting Head EVEN once, and then deducting it from total probability (1); this will assure that we get the Heads—one time, two times, and all three times.

   So, probability of getting at least one Head = 1 − (Probability of getting Tails in all 3 tosses)

   $= 1 - \left(\dfrac{1}{2} \cdot \dfrac{1}{2} \cdot \dfrac{1}{2} \right) = 1 - \dfrac{1}{8} = \dfrac{7}{8}$.

   The correct answer is option D.

3. Number of students = 36; Number of Boys = 18, so, number of girls = 18.

   Since the 3 selected students are boys, the number of boys remaining = 15. & total number of students remaining =33.

   So, the probability of selecting 4th boy $= \dfrac{\text{Number of Boys remaining}}{\text{Total no. of students remaining}} = 15/33 = 5/11$.

   The correct answer is option D.

   Remember that this question is different from a similar question: *...what is the probability that all the students selected are boys?* The difference is that in this question, 4 boys and no girl are to be chosen, while in the earlier one, 3 boys were already chosen, and only the 4th boy was to be chosen.

We will deal with this kind of question in subsequent questions.

4. Number of diplomats = 9; Number of Japanese = 3; & Number of Chinese = 6.

The probability of choosing at least 2 Japanese = P (Japanese = 2, Chinese = 1) + P (Japanese = 3, Chinese = none)

$$\Rightarrow \text{P (Japanese = 2, Chinese = 1)} = \frac{C_2^3 . C_1^6}{C_3^9} = \frac{C_1^3 . C_1^6}{C_3^9} = \frac{3.6}{\dfrac{9.8.7}{1.2.3}} = 3/14; [C_r^n = C_{n-r}^n]$$

$$\Rightarrow \text{P (Japanese = 3, Chinese = none)} = \frac{C_3^3}{C_3^9} = \frac{1}{\dfrac{9.8.7}{1.2.3}} = 1/84; [C_n^n = 1]$$

Hence, the probability of choosing at least 2 Japanese = 3/14 + 1/84 = 19/84

The correct answer is option C.

5. The problem will not be solved in only condition when none among John, Peter, and Harry is able to solve it. Even if one of them could crack it, the problem will be solved as they have to solve it collectively.

So, probability of not solving the problem = P(John could not solve it) × P(Peter could not solve it) × P(Harry could not solve it)

$$\Rightarrow (1 - \frac{4}{5}).(1 - \frac{2}{3}).(1 - \frac{3}{4}) = \frac{1}{5}.\frac{1}{3}.\frac{1}{4} = 1/60$$

The correct answer is option A.

6. Total number of players = 5;

Number of players apart from John and Harry = 3;

Probability of choosing both John and Harry (2 players) and only one among the rest

$$= \frac{C_2^2 . C_1^3}{C_3^5} = \frac{1.3}{\dfrac{5.4.3}{1.2.3}} = 3/10.$$

The correct answer is option C.

7. Total Number of actors = 5;

Since Jack and Steve need to be in the selection and Suzy is to be left out, only one selection matters.

Number of actors apart from Jack, Steve, and Suzy = 2;

Probability of choosing 3 actors including Jack and Steve, but not Suzy $= \dfrac{C_1^2}{C_3^5} = 1/5$

The correct answer is option A.

8. Number of silver coins = p; Number of gold coins = q; so total umber of coins = $p + q$;

The probability of getting 1st coin as silver coin and 2nd coin as gold coin = P (silver coin) $\times$ P (gold coin)

$\Rightarrow$ P (silver coin) $= \dfrac{C_1^p}{C_1^{p+q}} = \dfrac{p}{p + q}$

After 1st draw, there would be only $p + q - 1$ number of coins left.

$\Rightarrow$ So, P (gold coin) $= \dfrac{C_1^q}{C_1^{p+q-1}} = \dfrac{q}{p + q - 1}$

$\Rightarrow$ Hence, the probability of getting 1st coin as silver coin and 2nd coin as gold coin

$= \left(\dfrac{p}{p + q}\right)\left(\dfrac{q}{p + q - 1}\right)$

The correct answer is option D.

You could have solved this question by picking some values for p and q. Say $p = 2$ and $q = 4$; after solving, plug in the values of p and q in the options, and cross check which option matches the derived value. The derived value is 4/15 and matches with option D.

9. A number is divisible by 2, if it is an even number.

Between 100 and 400, there are 400 – 100 + 1 = 301 numbers. Out of these, 151 numbers are Even and 150 numbers are Odd.

So, the probability of winning a gift $= \dfrac{\text{Number of even numbered coupons}}{\text{Total number of coupons}} = 151/301$

The correct answer is option C.

10. Probability of choosing any paired husband from group A = 5/50 = 1/10;

The chosen husband will have only one married woman in group B as his wife. So, the probability of choosing paired wife = 1/40;

So, the probability of choosing a paired husband-wife = (1/10) $\times$ (1/40) = 1/400;

The correct answer is option A.

The answer (5/50) $\times$ (5/40) = 1/80 is wrong because choosing any husband from group 1 and any wife from group 2 will not necessarily make the correct husband-wife pair.

11. Probability of getting 1st ball being green = 10/30 = 1/3;

Since the ball drawn is replaced, the total number of balls would remain 30, the probability of getting 2nd ball as green = 10/30 = 1/3;

So, the probability of getting both the balls being green = (1/3).(1/3) = 1/9.

The correct answer is option B.

12. Say number of green balls are x, so the total number of balls = $(4 + x)$;

Number of ways both the ball drawn will be black = C_2^4;

Total number of ways 2 balls can be drawn = C_2^{4+x};

Hence, the probability of getting both the balls being black =

$$\frac{C_2^4}{C_2^{(4+x)}} = \frac{4.3/1.2}{(4+x).(3+x)/1.2} = \frac{1}{6} \text{ (given)};$$

This reduces to $\dfrac{4.3}{(4+x).(3+x)} = \dfrac{1}{6}$;

We do not recommend you to solve the quadratic equation to get the value of x, you must plug in the values of x from the options and check if right hand side and left hand side are equal. If yes, the option is the correct answer.

Trying with $x = 5$ will satisfy the equation as $\dfrac{4.3}{9.8} = \dfrac{1}{6} \Rightarrow \dfrac{1}{6} = \dfrac{1}{6}$.

The correct answer is option C.

13. As per the given information , 16 questions would be correct. For the remaining 25 questions, we will have to calculate the probability of getting them correct.

⇒ Probability of getting the 10 set of question with 2 unsure options = 1/2, so we can expect that the candidate will mark $10 \times 1/2 = 5$ questions correct.

⇒ Similarly, probability of getting the 6 set of question with 3 unsure options = 1/3, so we can expect that the candidate will mark $6 \times 1/3 = 2$ questions correct.

⇒ Similarly, probability of getting the 4 set of question with 4 unsure options = 1/4, so we can expect that the candidate will mark $4 \times 1/4 = 1$ question correct.

⇒ Similarly, probability of getting the 5 set of question with 5 unsure options = 1/5, so we can expect that the candidate will mark $5 \times 1/5 = 1$ question correct.

So, the number of questions can be marked correctly = 16 + 5 + 2 + 1 + 1 = 25.

The correct answer is option B.

14. The better approach would be to find out the probability of getting both the non-defective spanners, and then deduct the probability from '1' to get the answer. It will make sure that either one or both the spanners are defective.

So, the probability of getting both the non-defective spanners = $\dfrac{C_2^7}{C_2^{10}} = \dfrac{7.6/1.2}{10.9/1.2} = \dfrac{7}{15}$

Hence, the probability of getting at least one defective spanner = $1 - 7/15 = 8/15$

The correct answer is option D.

15. Number of students = 20; Number of boys = 15; hence, the number of girls = 5;

So, the probability of getting 1 boy and 2 girls = $\dfrac{C_1^{15}.C_2^5}{C_3^{20}} = \dfrac{(15/1).(5.4/1.2)}{20.19.18/1.2.3} = \dfrac{5}{38}.$

The correct answer is option A.

16. The meaning of 'all the 100 shots do not miss the target' is that at least one or all the 100 shots hit the target. It would be very time-consuming to calculate the answer if we follow the traditional approach as this involves handling of 100 terms. Let us do it in another way.

Let all the 100 shots miss and then we would deduct the derived value from '1' to get the answer.

Given that:

Probability that a shot hits the target = 1/100

Thus, probability that a shot misses the target = $1 - 1/100 = 99/100$

Probability that all the 100 shots miss the target $= \left(\dfrac{99}{100}\right)^{100}$

We need to determine the probability that ALL shots do not miss.

Required probability = 1 − P(All shots miss the target)

$= 1 - \left(\dfrac{99}{100}\right)^{100}$

$= \dfrac{(100^{100} - 99^{100})}{100^{100}}$

The correct answer is option D.

17. No. of people = 12, No. of Japanese = 3, No. of Australian = 4, & No. of Chinese = 5.

We must group Australians and Chinese to make one group of 9 people.

The probability of choosing 2 Japanese out of 4 people
= Probability (Japanese = 2, Australian + Chinese = 2)

$$\Rightarrow P\,(J = 2, A + C = 2) = \frac{C_2^3 \cdot C_2^9}{C_4^{12}} = \frac{(3.2/1.2).(9.8/1.2)}{\dfrac{12.11.10.9}{1.2.3.4}} = 12/55;$$

The correct answer is option B.

18. Probability of losing the bet each day = 0.4. It means that the probability of winning the bet each day = 1 − 0.4 = 0.6.

Probability (Winning = 2 days)
= (Number of ways any 2 chosen winning days) × (Probability of winning on 2 days, and losing on the other day)
= $[C_2^3].[(0.6).(0.6).(0.4)] = 0.432;$

The correct answer is option D.

19. Since the cards with digits (0, 3, 4, 9) are already drawn, the cards with 1, 2, 5, 6, 7, 8 digits are remaining in the box, i.e., a total of 6 cards; out of which cards with digits (1, 5, 7) are with odd integers: 3 cards.

We have to draw 2 cards out of these 3 cards.

The probability = $\dfrac{C_2^3}{C_2^6} = \dfrac{\dfrac{3.2}{1.2}}{\dfrac{6.5}{1.2}} = \dfrac{1}{5}$

The correct answer is option B.

20. Let us solve the inequality $|2x - 3| > 3$.

$|2x - 3| > 3 \Rightarrow 2x - 3 > 3 \Rightarrow 2x > 3 + 3 \Rightarrow 2x > 6 \Rightarrow x > 3.$ Values $(4, 6)$ from the set satisfy the inequality.

or,

$|2x - 3| > 3 \Rightarrow 2x - 3 < -3 \Rightarrow 2x < -3 + 3 \Rightarrow 2x < 0 \Rightarrow x < 0.$ Values $(-6, -4, -2)$ from the set satisfy the inequality.

So a total of 5 values out of 7 satisfy the inequality. The probability = 5/7.

The correct answer is option D.

21. Probability of a missile hitting a target = 0.6.

Thus, probability of the missile missing the target = 0.4.

Calculating 'the probability of hitting the target at least once' with the traditional approach would be time-consuming. The only possibility that is NOT desired is: No missile hits the target. Subtracting not-desired probability form '1', will give us the answer.

For three missiles, the probability that all three miss the target = $0.4 \times 0.4 \times 0.4 = 0.064$.

Thus, probability that at least one missile hits the target

= 1 – (Probability that all three missiles miss the target) = $1 - 0.064 = 0.936$.

The correct answer is option C.

22. Among integers from 1 to 100, the numbers which are odd perfect squares are 1, 9, 25, 49, and 81; i.e. there are five such numbers.

We can select two of them in C_2^5 ways.

We can select two numbers from the 100 numbers (1 to 100) in C_2^{100} ways.

Thus, required probability $= \dfrac{C_2^5}{C_2^{100}} = \dfrac{\dfrac{(5 \times 4)}{(2 \times 1)}}{\dfrac{(100 \times 99)}{(2 \times 1)}} = \dfrac{5 \times 4}{100 \times 99} = \dfrac{1}{495}$.

The correct answer is option B.

23. From numbers 1 to 50, the primes are: 2, 3, 5, 7, 11, 13, 17, 19, 23, 29, 31, 37, 41, 43, and 47; i.e. there are 15 prime numbers.

The perfect squares are: 1, 4, 9, 16, 25, 36 and 49; i.e. there are 7 perfect squares.

There is no perfect square which can also be a prime.

Thus, since we want a number which is neither a prime nor a perfect square, we have to exclude $15 + 7 = 22$ numbers.

Thus, there are $50 - 22 = 28$ desired numbers.

We can select 2 of these in C_2^{28} ways.

We can select 2 of the 50 numbers in C_2^{50} ways.

Thus, required probability $= \dfrac{C_2^{28}}{C_2^{50}} = \dfrac{\dfrac{28 \times 27}{2 \times 1}}{\dfrac{50 \times 49}{2 \times 1}} = \dfrac{28 \times 27}{50 \times 49} = 0.308 = \approx 0.31$.

The correct answer is option C.

24. Three balls of different colors imply one white, one red and one blue ball.

These may be selected in C_1^4, C_1^3 and C_1^3 ways respectively.

However, their drawings can be done in 3! = 6 ways.

There are a total of 4 + 3 + 3 = 10 balls.

Ways of selecting three balls successively without replacement = $C_1^{10} \times C_1^9 \times C_1^8$.

Thus, required probability = $\dfrac{6 \times C_1^4 \times C_1^3 \times C_1^3}{C_1^{10} \times C_1^9 \times C_1^8} = \dfrac{6 \times 4 \times 3 \times 3}{10 \times 9 \times 8} = \dfrac{3}{10}$.

The correct answer is option A.

25. We can select balls of the same color if the balls are either both white or both black.

Thus, the necessary condition is:

- The ball from 1st bag is white AND that from 2nd bag is also white

    OR

- The ball from 1st bag is black AND that from 2nd bag is also black

Thus, required probability = $\dfrac{C_1^3 \times C_1^4}{C_1^5 \times C_1^9} + \dfrac{C_1^2 \times C_1^5}{C_1^5 \times C_1^9} = \dfrac{3 \times 4}{5 \times 9} + \dfrac{2 \times 5}{5 \times 9} = \dfrac{12}{45} + \dfrac{10}{45} = \dfrac{22}{45}$.

The correct answer is option B.

26. A blue ball can be drawn only if a ball is drawn from the first box as the second box does not have blue balls.

Thus, the only condition is: Heads appears AND a blue ball is drawn.

Probability of a Head appearing = $\dfrac{1}{2}$.

Probability of drawing a blue ball = $\dfrac{C_1^3}{C_1^{(3+2)}} = \dfrac{C_1^3}{C_1^5} = \dfrac{3}{5}$.

Thus, required probability = $\dfrac{1}{2} \times \dfrac{3}{5} = \dfrac{3}{10} = 0.3$.

The correct answer is option C.

27. For a normal die, the probability of each number appearing is the same, equal to $\frac{1}{6}$.

However, here, their probabilities are different.

Let the probability of each odd number appearing = p.

Thus, the probability of each even number appearing = $2p$.

We know that sum of probabilities of all possible cases is 1.

Since there are three odd and three even numbers, we have:

$$p + p + p + 2p + 2p + 2p = 1 \Rightarrow 9p = 1 \Rightarrow p = 1/9.$$

Thus, probability of each odd number = $p = \frac{1}{9}$.

Also, probability of each even number = $2p = \frac{2}{9}$.

Thus, probability of getting consecutive 6s (even number) on two throws of this dice = $\frac{2}{9} \times \frac{2}{9} = \frac{4}{81}$.

The correct answer is option C.

28. The ball would all be of the same color if all three are yellow OR all are green.

Thus, probability = $\dfrac{C_3^5}{C_3^9} + \dfrac{C_3^4}{C_3^9} = \dfrac{\frac{5 \times 4 \times 3}{3!}}{\frac{9 \times 8 \times 7}{3!}} + \dfrac{\frac{4 \times 3 \times 2}{3!}}{\frac{9 \times 8 \times 7}{3!}} = \dfrac{10}{84} + \dfrac{4}{84} = \dfrac{14}{84} = \dfrac{1}{6}$.

Thus, probability that balls are not all of the same color = $1 - \dfrac{1}{6} = \dfrac{5}{6} = 0.83$.

Alternatively, since the balls are not all of the same color, there are only two possible cases:

(1) Two yellow AND one green

   OR

(2) Two green AND one yellow

Hence, required probability = $\dfrac{C_2^5 \times C_1^4}{C_3^9} + \dfrac{C_1^5 \times C_2^4}{C_3^9} = \dfrac{10 \times 4}{84} + \dfrac{5 \times 6}{84} = \dfrac{70}{84} = \dfrac{5}{6}$.

The correct answer is option C.

29. **Traditional approach:**

- $A = \dfrac{C_2^{12}}{C_2^{22}} = \dfrac{12.11}{22.21} \times \dfrac{1.2}{1.2} = \dfrac{2}{7}$

- $B = \dfrac{C_2^{10}}{C_2^{22}} = \dfrac{10.9}{22.21} \times \dfrac{1.2}{1.2} = \dfrac{15}{77}$

We can rewrite $A = \dfrac{2}{7} = \dfrac{22}{77}$, thus A > B; or options A and E are wrong.

- $C = \dfrac{C_1^{12} . C_1^{10}}{C_2^{22}} = \dfrac{12.10}{22.21} \times 2 = \dfrac{40}{77}$

So, the answer is $C > A > B$.

The correct answer is option D.

Logical deduction approach:

Since A = Probability of drawing two **red** balls from a bag containing 12 red and 10 blue balls, and B = Probability of drawing two **blue** balls from a bag containing 12 red and 10 blue balls, value of A would be greater than B as there are two more red balls compared to blue balls; so, A > B.

Again, C = Probability of drawing **one red and one blue** ball from a bag containing 12 red and 10 blue balls, value of C would be greater than A and greater than B as in case of C, there are more chances **one red and one blue**, versus **both red** and **both blue**; so, C > A > B.

30. Total number of arrangements possible = 4!

If A is to the immediate left of C, we make AC (in this order) as one unit. Thus, there are now three things to arrange which can be done in 3! ways.

Hence, required probability $= \dfrac{3!}{4!} = \dfrac{1}{4}$.

The correct answer is option B.

31. Since we do not want balls of the same color, we need to draw one red AND one blue ball.

We can select one red and one blue ball in C_1^{10} and C_1^{20} ways respectively.

We can select two balls from the 30 balls in C_2^{30} ways.

Thus, required probability $= \dfrac{C_1^{10} \times C_1^{20}}{C_2^{30}} = \dfrac{10 \times 20}{\dfrac{30 \times 29}{2}} = \dfrac{10 \times 20}{15 \times 39} = \dfrac{40}{87} =\approx 0.46$

The correct answer is option D.

32.   Since $x^2 \leq 16$, we can see that from the numbers in the given set, '-2', '0', '2' and '4' satisfy:

- $(-2)^2 = 4 < 16$ (qualifies)

- $0^2 = 0 < 16$ (qualifies)

- $2^2 = 4 < 16$ (qualifies)

- $4^2 = 16$ (qualifies)

- $6^2 = 36 > 16$ (does not qualify)

Thus, there are four favorable values of x out of the five values in the set.

Hence, required probability $= \dfrac{4}{5}$.

The correct answer is option D.

33.   We know that, probability of A **and** B $= P(A) \times P(B)$, provided A and B are independent

Here, the number appearing on each throw is not important.

Thus, the number on the first throw should repeat in each of the remaining two throws.

Thus, required probability

= Probability of getting any number in the 1st throw **and** probability of getting the same number in the 2nd throw **and** probability of getting the same number in the 3rd throw

$= 1 \times \dfrac{1}{6} \times \dfrac{1}{6} = \dfrac{1}{36}$

(Since there are six faces in a dice, the probability of a particular number appearing is $\dfrac{1}{6}$).

The correct answer is option A.

Alternate Approach 1:

When a die is thrown thrice, there are $6 \times 6 \times 6 = 216$ possibilities; out of which, we are interested in $(1,1,1), (2,2,2), (3,3,3), (4,4,4), (5,5,5)$, and $(6,6,6)$: 6 ways.

Thus, required probability $= \dfrac{6}{216} = \dfrac{1}{36}$.

Alternate Approach 2:

Let us take the case of a number '1' appearing thrice:

Probability of getting '1' three times in a row = $\dfrac{1}{6} \times \dfrac{1}{6} \times \dfrac{1}{6} = \dfrac{1}{216}$

Similarly, the probabilities of getting each of '2, 3, 4, 5, & 6' three times in a row = $\dfrac{1}{216}$

Thus, required probability = $6 \times \dfrac{1}{216} = \dfrac{1}{36}$.

34. We know that,

Probability of A **or** B = P (A) + P (B) − P(A ∩ B)

There are three odd numbers: 1, 3, & 5 and there are three prime numbers: 2, 3, & 5.

There are two numbers which are both odd as well as prime: 3 & 5.

Thus, required probability = P (odd) + P (prime) − P (odd and prime)

$= \dfrac{3}{6} + \dfrac{3}{6} - \dfrac{2}{6} = \dfrac{4}{6} = \dfrac{2}{3}$.

The correct answer is option C.

35. There are a total of 6 × 6 = 36 cases when a dice is thrown twice.

Of these, there are six cases when the throws give the same number.

Thus, there are 36 − 6 = 30 cases where the numbers on the two faces are different.

Of these 30 cases, it is obvious that half the cases i.e. 15 would have the number on the first throw greater than the other and similarly 15 more for the other way round.

Thus, required probability = $\dfrac{15}{36} = \dfrac{5}{12}$.

The correct answer is option B.

36. There are five cards numbered '1' to '5'.

Thus, two cards (same card can now be used twice) which add up to eight could be (5, 3); (3, 5) or (4, 4).

Thus, required probability = Probability of getting

- 1st card = 5 and 2nd card = 3

OR

- 1st card = 3 and 2nd card = 5

    OR

- 1st card = 4 and 2nd card = 4

$$= \frac{1}{5} \times \frac{1}{5} + \frac{1}{5} \times \frac{1}{5} \times \frac{1}{5} \times \frac{1}{5} = \frac{3}{25}.$$

The correct answer is option A.

37. We know that,

Probability of an event = 1 - Probability of the event not occurring

Let us find the probability that '3' does not occur even once on throwing a dice thrice.

A traditional approach would be to solve the question by calculating the probabilities of getting '3' once, and then twice, and thereafter adding them; however it would be time-consuming.

An optimum approach would be to calculate the probability of not getting '3' even once and then deducting the compound probability from 1.

So, probability of not getting a '3' on throwing a dice once = $1 - \frac{1}{6} = \frac{5}{6}$.

Thus, probability of not getting a '3' on throwing a dice twice = $\frac{5}{6} \times \frac{5}{6} = \frac{25}{36}$.

Thus, probability of getting '3' at least once = $1 - \frac{25}{36} = \frac{11}{36}$.

The correct answer is option C.

38. We know that,

Probability of an event = $\dfrac{\text{Favorable cases}}{\text{Total cases}}$

Mean = $\dfrac{\text{Sum of all terms}}{\text{\# of terms}}$

The mean of the numbers in the set = $\dfrac{1 + 2 + 2 + 3 + 4 + 5 + 5 + 5 + 9}{9} = \dfrac{36}{9} = 4$.

The term 4 is present only once in the set which has 9 terms.

Hence, required probability = $\frac{1}{9}$.

The correct answer is option C.

39.   The possible cases where one number from A and one from B add up to 9 are:
(1, 8) and (6, 3).

Thus, there are two favorable cases.

Total number of ways of selecting one number from A and one from B = 3 × 3 = 9.

Hence, required probability = $\frac{2}{9}$.

The correct answer is option B.

40.   The possible cases where one number from A and one from B when multiplied give 9 is: (3, 3).

Thus, there is one favorable cases.

Total number of ways of selecting one number from A and one from B = 3 × 3 = 9.

Hence, required probability = $\frac{1}{9}$.

The correct answer is option C.

41.   We know that,

P (A) + P($\overline{\text{A}}$) = 1; where P($\overline{\text{A}}$) is the probability of the event A not happening

Probability of picking a red ball = P (Red)

= 1 − [P (Blue) + P (Green)]

= $1 - \left[\frac{1}{4} + \frac{2}{3}\right] = \frac{1}{12} = \frac{2}{24}$.

Hence, number of red balls

= (Total number of balls) × P (Red)

= $24 \times \frac{2}{24} = 2$.

The correct answer is option B.

42. Let us calculate A.

We know that probability of head = $\frac{1}{2}$.

Hence, required probability of all heads = $\left(\frac{1}{2} \times \frac{1}{2} \times \frac{1}{2}\right) = \frac{1}{8}$

Similarly, B = probability of all tails = $\left(\frac{1}{2} \times \frac{1}{2} \times \frac{1}{2}\right) = \frac{1}{8}$

So, A = B; it means that options A and b are wrong.

Let us calculate C.

C = Probability of getting two heads and one tail = $C_1^3 \times \left(\frac{1}{2} \times \frac{1}{2} \times \frac{1}{2}\right) = \frac{3}{8}$;

$C_1^3 = 3$ is the number of ways in which two heads may appear out of three tosses: [1st & 2nd]; [1st & 3rd]; [2nd & 3rd]

Thus, $C = 3A = 3B$

The correct answer is option D.

43. Probability of an event = $\dfrac{\text{Number of favorable events}}{\text{Number of total events}}$;

Here, number of favorable events = number of ways 2 green balls can be selected from 10 balls = C_2^{10};

Number of total events = number of ways 2 balls can be selected from 30 balls = C_2^{30}

Hence, probability of getting both the green balls = $\dfrac{C_2^{10}}{C_2^{30}} = \dfrac{10.9/1.2}{30.29/1.2} = \dfrac{3}{29}$;

The correct answer is option A.

44. Since the coin is unbiased, it means that probabilities of getting a 'Head' or getting a 'Tail' upon a single toss are equal = 1/2.

Traditional approach of solving this question would be to find the probability for each time the coin turns Head and then add them, but that is a lengthy process.

An efficient approach would be to find out the probability of not getting Head EVEN once, and then deducting it from total probability (1); this will assure that we get the Heads—one time, two times, and all three times.

So, probability of getting at least one Head = 1 − (Probability of getting Tails in all 3 tosses)

$= 1 - \left(\frac{1}{2}.\frac{1}{2}.\frac{1}{2}\right) = 1 - \frac{1}{8} = \frac{7}{8}$.

The correct answer is option D.

45. The problem will not be solved in only condition when none among John, Peter, and Harry is able to solve it. Even if one of them could crack it, the problem will be solved as they have to solve it collectively.

So, probability of not solving the problem = P(John could not solve it) × P(Peter could not solve it) × P(Harry could not solve it)

$$\Rightarrow (1 - \frac{4}{5}).(1 - \frac{2}{3}).(1 - \frac{3}{4}) = \frac{1}{5}.\frac{1}{3}.\frac{1}{4} = 1/60$$

The correct answer is option A.

46. Total Number of actors = 5;

Since Jack and Steve need to be in the selection and Suzy is to be left out, only one selection matters.

Number of actors apart from Jack, Steve, and Suzy = 2;

Probability of choosing 3 actors including Jack and Steve, but not Suzy = $\dfrac{C_1^2}{C_3^5} = 1/5$

The correct answer is option A.

47. Number of silver coins = p; Number of gold coins = q; so total umber of coins = $p + q$;

The probability of getting 1st coin a silver coin as well as 2nd coin a silver coin = P (silver coin I) × P (silver coin II)

$$\Rightarrow \text{P (silver coin I)} = \frac{C_1^p}{C_1^{p+q}} = \frac{p}{p+q}$$

After 1st draw, there would be only $p + q - 1$ number of coins left.

$$\Rightarrow \text{So, P (silver coin II)} = \frac{C_1^{p-1}}{C_1^{p+q-1}} = \frac{p-1}{p+q-1}$$

$\Rightarrow$ Hence, the probability of getting 1st coin a silver coin as well as 2nd coin a silver coin =

$$\left(\frac{p}{p+q} \right) \left(\frac{p-1}{p+q-1} \right) = \frac{p(p-1)}{(p+q)(p+q-1)}$$

The correct answer is option B.

You could have solved this question by picking some values for p and q. Say $p = 2$ and $q = 4$; after solving, plug in the values of p and q in the options, and cross check which option matches the derived value. The derived value is 1/15 and matches with option B.

48. A number is divisible by 2, if it is an even number.

Between 100 and 400, there are 400 − 100 + 1 = 301 numbers. Out of these, 151 numbers are Even and 150 numbers are Odd.

So, the probability of winning a gift = $\dfrac{\text{Number of even numbered coupons}}{\text{Total number of coupons}}$

= 151/301

The correct answer is option C.

49. Say number of green balls are x, so the total number of balls = $(4 + x)$;

Number of ways both the ball drawn will be black = C_2^4;

Total number of ways 2 balls can be drawn = C_2^{4+x};

Hence, the probability of getting both the balls being black =

$\dfrac{C_2^4}{C_2^{(4+x)}} = \dfrac{4.3/1.2}{(4+x).(3+x)/1.2} = \dfrac{1}{6}$ (given);

This reduces to $\dfrac{4.3}{(4+x).(3+x)} = \dfrac{1}{6}$;

We do not recommend you to solve the quadratic equation to get the value of x, you must plug in the values of x from the options and check if right hand side and left hand side are equal. If yes, the option is the correct answer.

Trying with $x = 5$ will satisfy the equation as $\dfrac{4.3}{9.8} = \dfrac{1}{6} \Rightarrow \dfrac{1}{6} = \dfrac{1}{6}$.

The correct answer is option C.

50. Probability of hitting the triangle = $\dfrac{\text{Area of the triangle}}{\text{Area of the triangle \& areas of three semi-circles}}$

Area of the equilateral triangle = $\dfrac{\sqrt{3}}{4}$side$^2 = \dfrac{\sqrt{3}}{4}.4^2 = 4\sqrt{3}$

Area of the three semi-circles = $3(\dfrac{1}{2}.\pi r^2) = \dfrac{3}{2}.2^2.\pi = 6\pi$; Radius = half of side
= 4/2 = 2 cm.

Total area of dartboard = $4\sqrt{3} + 6\pi$

Thus, the probability of hitting the triangular part = $\dfrac{4\sqrt{3}}{4\sqrt{3} + 6\pi}$

The correct answer is option D.

10.2   Student-Produced Response or Grid-In Questions

51. We know that the probability of getting a Head or a Tail on any toss of a coin = 1/2.

Say we get Head on the first toss, and all Tails on the next 5 tosses of the coin,

$$=> P(H_1, T_{2,3,4,5,6}) = (1/2) \times (1/2 \times 1/2 \times 1/2 \times 1/2 \times 1/2) = (1/2)^6 = 1/64$$

Similarly, we can get Head on $2^{nd}, 3^{rd}, 4^{th}, 5^{th}$, or 6th trials. Thus, there are six possibilities.

So, $P(1H, 5T) = 6 \times (1/2)^6 = 3/32$

3	/	3	2

52. We have seen the following table in the theory part; let's revisit it.

Sum	Ways	Number of ways	Frequency distribution & Probabilities
2	{1,1}	1	$p = \dfrac{1}{36}$
3	{2,1}, {1,2}	2	$p = \dfrac{1}{18}$
4	{3,1}, {2,2}, {1,3}	3	$p = \dfrac{1}{12}$
5	{4,1}, {3,2}, {2,3}, {1,4}	4	$p = \dfrac{1}{9}$
6	{5,1}, {4,2}, {3,3}, {2,4}, {1,5}	5	$p = \dfrac{5}{36}$
7	{6,1}, {5,2}, {4,3}, {3,4}, {2,5}, {1,6}	6	$p = \dfrac{1}{6}$
8	{6,2}, {5,3}, {4,4}, {3,5}, {2,6}	5	$p = \dfrac{5}{36}$
9	{6,3}, {5,4}, {4,5}, {3,6}	4	$p = \dfrac{1}{9}$
10	{6,4}, {5,5}, {4,6}	3	$p = \dfrac{1}{12}$
11	{6,5}, {5,6}	2	$p = \dfrac{1}{18}$
12	{6,6}	1	$p = \dfrac{1}{36}$
	Total number of ways	36	

Memorise...

1. If Sum ≤ 7, then Number of ways = Sum − 1

2. If Sum ≥ 8, then Number of ways = 13 − Sum

We have to calculate the probability of getting the sum > 9. It would be

$$\Rightarrow P(\text{SUM} > 9) = \frac{n\{\text{\# of ways of getting a sum of 10, 11, or 12}\}}{36} = \frac{3+2+1}{36} = 1/6$$

1	/	6	

53. $P(I > 2, II > 3, III > 4) = P(I > 2) \times P(II > 3) \times P(III > 4) = (4/6) \times (3/6) \times (2/6) = 1/9$

1	/	9	

54. We have to find out the probability that Aleck and Chris will watch the NBA final but Ben will not.

Given: $P(A) = 1/4, P(B) = 1/3, P(\overline{C}) = 1/2$

$\Rightarrow$ P(Aleck, Ben, Chris) $= P(A, \overline{B}, C) = P(A) \times P(\overline{B}) \times P(C)$
$= 1/4 \times (1 - 1/3) \times (1 - 1/2) = 1/4 \times 2/3 \times 1/2 = 1/12.$

1	/	1	2

55. Probability of choosing 2 boys $= \dfrac{\text{\# of ways of choosing 2 boys out of 10 boys}}{\text{\# of ways of choosing 2 students out of 20 (10 + 10) students}}$

Probability of choosing 2 boys $= \dfrac{C_2^{10}}{C_2^{22}} = \dfrac{\frac{10.9}{1.2}}{\frac{20.19}{1.2}} = 9/38.$

9	/	3	8

56. Probability of choosing 2 boys or 2 girls

$= \dfrac{\text{\# of ways of choosing [2 boys out of 10 boys + 2 girls out of 12 girls]}}{\text{\# of ways of choosing 2 students out of 22 students}}$

Probability of choosing 2 boys or 2 girls $= \dfrac{C_2^{10} + C_2^{12}}{C_2^{22}} = \dfrac{\frac{10.9}{1.2} + \frac{12.11}{1.2}}{\frac{22.21}{1.2}} = 37/77 = 0.48.$

Hence the correct answer is $37/77 = 0.48$ or $.480$ or $.481$.

If the selection considered both the boys or both the girls, then why is the probability $\neq 1$? It is 0.48, nearly 50%! When we know that if all the events are taken into consideration, the sum of probabilities of all the events is 1. This means that at at least one event is left to be considered.

And that event is: Selection of 1 boy and 1 girl.

It means that the probability of choosing 1 boys AND 1 girls must be equal to $1 - 0.48 = 0.52$.

Let us cross check.

Probability of choosing 1 boys AND 1 girls = $\dfrac{C_1^{10} \times C_1^{12}}{C_2^{22}} = \dfrac{10 \times 12}{\dfrac{22.21}{1.2}} = 40/77 = 0.52$, (the desired

answer).

| 0 | . | 4 | 8 |

57. Number of students who play Soccer, Basketball or both = 120 − 30 = 90.

Since 68 play Soccer, and 48 play Basketball, making a total of 116 [68+48], it means that 116 − 90 = 26 play both Soccer and Basketball.

Or, 68 − 26 = 42 play only Soccer, and hence the probability of picking a student, playing only Soccer = 42/120 = 7/20.

| 7 | / | 2 | 0 |

58. The question is different from the previous one. Here, we have to pick a student out of the pool of 68 students (who play Soccer) and not from all the students, 120, as was the case in the previous questions.

Thus, the probability of picking a student, playing only Soccer given that they play Soccer = 42/68 = 21/34 = 0.618.

Hence the correct answer is 0.62 or .618.

Take Away: Read questions carefully; denominator does not always take ALL.

| 0 | . | 6 | 2 |

Following two questions are based on the table.

Employees during the year 2014-2015			
Employees	Permanent	Temporary	Total
Male	80	30	110
Female	30	40	70
Total	110	70	180

59. Given the constraint in the question, we have to find out the probability of choosing an employee being a male out of all the permanent employees (110), and not out of all the employees, 180.

We find that out of all the permanent employees (110), 80 males, so the probability = 80/110 = 8/11.

8	/	1	1

60. The company wishes to increase the headcount of female employees to 105 in the year 2015-16, keeping the same proportion of permanent to temporary employees. It means that the probability of choosing a permanent females employees among total females (30/70 = 3/7) in the year 2014-15 will remain the same in the year 2015-16.

Thus, # of females employees in the year 2015-16 = Probability of choosing a permanent female employee among total females (105) = (3/7) × 105 = 45.

4	5		

61. Probability of hitting the gray part = $\dfrac{\text{Area of the gray part}}{\text{Area of the outermost circle}}$

Say the radius of the inner circle = r

So, area of the inner circle = πr^2

Area of the middle circle = $\pi (2r)^2 = 4\pi r^2$

So, area of the gray part = Area of the middle circle – Area of the inner circle
$$= 4\pi r^2 - \pi r^2 = 3\pi r^2$$

Area of the outermost circle = $\pi (3r)^2 = 9\pi r^2$

Thus, the probability of hitting the gray area = $\dfrac{3\pi r^2}{9\pi r^2} = 1/3$

1	/	3	

62. Probability of picking both the spanners being defective = $\dfrac{C_2^x}{C_2^{10}} = \dfrac{2}{15}$ (given)

$$\Rightarrow \dfrac{\dfrac{x.(x-1)}{1.2}}{\dfrac{10.9}{1.2}} = \dfrac{x.(x-1)}{10.9} = \dfrac{2}{15}$$

$$\Rightarrow x(x-1) = \dfrac{2.10.9}{15}$$

$$\Rightarrow x(x-1) = \dfrac{2.\cancel{10}2.\cancel{9}3}{\cancel{15}\cancel{3}1} = 12$$

Upon simplifying, we get $x.(x-1) = 12$

$$\Rightarrow x.(x-1) = 4.3 \Rightarrow x = 4 \text{ (Product of two consecutive integers)}.$$

Alternatively, you can get the value of x upon solving a quadratic equation. Let's see how.

$x.(x-1) = 12$

$=> x^2 - x - 12 = 0 => x^2 - 4x + 3x - 12 = 0 => x(x-4) + 3(x-4) = 0$

$=> (x-4)(x+3) = 0 => x = 4$ or $x = -3$.

Since x, spanners, cannot be negative, we reject a flawed value –3, so $x = 4$.

63. Probability of drawing a green ball $= \dfrac{\text{Drawing a green ball}}{\text{Total \# of balls}}$

We do not know the actual # of balls, however it cannot stop us from calculating the probability since the ratio values are given.

Given that:

Red : Yellow : Green balls
47 :   37 :
        148 :   67

We cannot use the ratio figures right away as we want the ratio of **Red : Yellow : Green** balls, which is not given, however we can compute it.

As per the ratio value, Yellow balls are either 37 or 148; since the LCM of 37 & 148 is 148;

Let's take the value 148; so the ratio of Red : Yellow :: 47 : 37 must be multiplied by a factor of '4' as 148/37 = 4.

Thus, Red : Yellow :: 47 : 37 => Red : Yellow :: $(4 \times 47) : (4 \times 37)$

=> Red : Yellow :: 188 : 148. Now we can calculate the combined ratio of Red : Yellow : Green balls.

=> **Red : Yellow : Green :: 188 : 148 : 67**

Say a common factor in the ratio of Red : Yellow : Green balls is x,

Thus, # of Green balls = $67x$

And, total # of balls = $(188 + 148 + 67)x = 403x$

So, the probability of drawing a green ball $= \dfrac{67x}{403x} = \dfrac{67}{403} = 0.17$ or .166

64. Since either of x or y is a positive integer less than 5, the possible values of one of the variables for $x + y = 5$ would be one among $\{1, 2, 3, 4\}$. This results in the value of the other variable equals one among $\{4, 3, 2, 1\}$.

So, in any case, $x \geq 1$, hence $P(x \geq 1) = 1$.

1			

65. We know that the probability of getting a Head or a Tail on any toss for a coin = 1/2.

We want Head, Head, Tail (in this order) on three tosses,

so the probability of getting HHT = $(1/2) \times (1/2) \times (1/2) = 1/8$.

Hence the correct answer is 1/8.

This question is different from a question asking for getting two Heads and a Tail. In this case, one can get two Heads in I & II, or I & III, or in II & III positions. The answer would have been $3 \times 1/8 = 3/8$.

1		/	8

66. We have seen the following table in the theory part; let's revisit it.

Sum	Ways	Number of ways	Frequency distribution & Probabilities
2	{1,1}	1	$p = \dfrac{1}{36}$
3	{2,1}, {1,2}	2	$p = \dfrac{1}{18}$
4	{3,1}, {2,2}, {1,3}	3	$p = \dfrac{1}{12}$
5	{4,1}, {3,2}, {2,3}, {1,4}	4	$p = \dfrac{1}{9}$
6	{5,1}, {4,2}, {3,3}, {2,4}, {1,5}	5	$p = \dfrac{5}{36}$
7	{6,1}, {5,2}, {4,3}, {3,4}, {2,5}, {1,6}	6	$p = \dfrac{1}{6}$
8	{6,2}, {5,3}, {4,4}, {3,5}, {2,6}	5	$p = \dfrac{5}{36}$
9	{6,3}, {5,4}, {4,5}, {3,6}	4	$p = \dfrac{1}{9}$
10	{6,4}, {5,5}, {4,6}	3	$p = \dfrac{1}{12}$
11	{6,5}, {5,6}	2	$p = \dfrac{1}{18}$
12	{6,6}	1	$p = \dfrac{1}{36}$
	Total number of ways	36	

Memorise...

1. If Sum $\leq$ 7, then Number of ways = Sum – 1

2. If Sum $\geq$ 8, then Number of ways = 13 – Sum

We have to calculate the probability of getting the sum > 10. It would be

$$P(\text{SUM} > 10) = \frac{n\{\text{\# of ways of getting a sum of 11 or 12}\}}{36} = \frac{2+1}{36} = 1/12$$

1	/	1	2

67. We know that the probability of getting a Head or a Tail on any toss for a coin = 1/2.

We want Head, Head, Tail (in this order) on three tosses,

so the probability of getting HHT = $(1/2) \times (1/2) \times (1/2) = 1/8$.

Hence the correct answer is 1/8.

This question is different from a question asking for getting two Heads and a Tail. In this case, one can get two Heads in I & II, or I & III, or in II & III positions. The answer would have been $3 \times 1/8 = 3/8$.

3	/	8	

68. $P(I > 2, II > 3, III > 4) = P(I > 2) \times P(II > 3) \times P(III > 4) = (4/6) \times (3/6) \times (2/6) = 1/9$

1	/	9	

69. $P(I > 2, II > 3, III > 4, IV > 5) = P(I > 2) \times P(II > 3) \times P(III > 4) \times P(IV > 5)$
    $= (4/6) \times (3/6) \times (2/6) \times (1/6) = 1/54$

1	/	5	4

Chapter 11

Talk to Us

Have a Question?

Email your questions to info@manhattanreview.com. We will be happy to answer you. Your questions can be related to a concept, an application of a concept, an explanation of a question, a suggestion for an alternate approach, or anything else you wish to ask regarding the SAT.

Please do mention the page number when quoting from the book.

Best of luck!

Happy Learning!

Professor Dr. Joern Meissner
& The Manhattan Review Team

Made in the USA
Lexington, KY
04 March 2018